# BUILD OR
# **DESTROY**

## "A Guide to Grinding"

ANTHONY R. BARBER JR

ISBN: 1-951047-02-8
ISBN: 9 781951 047023

Dedicated To My Grandmother
"Mildred A.k.a Boss Lady"
R.I.P

# CONTENTS

# BUILD OR
# **DESTROY**

# INTRODUCTION

I N THIS BOOK, I'll express to you, the reader, various methods and strategies I refer to as the "Build Philosophy." Examples and perspectives are given that outline ways and methods of achieving success – success as *you* view it, as it applies to *your life*. When I decided to write this book, I felt like the world, or at least my generation, had been spared the harsh reality of modern-day slavery in terms of how we've been conditioned to believe it to be, as-in the nine-to-five work-for-others-until-you-die philosophy.

My promise to you, the reader, is to simply offer perspective within these pages, along with examples of the various ways you can grind to achieve your true purpose. Some of the things I express in this book are easy to understand, and you're likely to agree with those messages right away. Other examples I offer might be totally dismissed by you as trash at first, only for you to find them relevant later to the way you choose to live your life.

I am not a psychic or seer or know-it-all guru. I'm an entre-preneur, investor, hustler, and a bit of a workaholic who has figured out the meaning of some of life's hidden truths. And I have decided to share my inside view of the inside view of forward-thinking.

This book is intended to be read as if you're having a conversation with a blunt, honest friend who, frankly, gives a damn about your happiness and wellbeing. I promise to turn your current grind and work ethic on its ear. I promise to challenge your status quo and crash the hardwired defeatist mentality you might possess.

The question I pose to you is this: What do you have to lose by gaining insight or perspective into what I call "grinding?" In simpler terms, grinding is nothing more than a desire to be free from mediocrity – so much so that you can go against traditional thinking and gain the life you were born to live. Within these pages, I will show you base comparisons of how dynamic the grind is, as well as examples of strange similarities shared on this very planet by a CEO, nature, animals, and even a pimp. It is very important that you, the reader, realize how closely everything relates to everything else; it's just a matter of how much truth you really want to live for. "It is as it truly is."

This book is for you if...

- You grew up in a restricted family or household.
- You march to the beat of your own drum.
- You're tired of feeling like you deserve more out of life.
- You have ever been told "no" and foolishly accepted it.
- You lack motivation…. need your fire lit.
- You want to move up in your career.
- You're an entrepreneur and you've lost your fire.
- You have talent (and know it) …but lack drive.
- You're simply tired of feeling like there's more…and want to get more.
- You're finished with excuses, and READY TO boss up.

I know what you're thinking...what exactly makes me an expert on grinding and being successful?

Answer: Nothing at all. As I stated, I'm no guru or mystic. I haven't had the privilege of living eighty-plus years on the planet, so I won't be trying to flex my existence on you like others likely have and will. I'm just a reasonably young man who has been through some things and bumped my head more than I care to mention. But along the way, I've figured out some things, and I've had many successes because of my willingness to experiment and step outside my fears directly into the creative fire of life. In this book, I'll give you a brief bird's eye view of what I've been through, seen, and experienced.

Some of my oldest, clearest memories are the stories my uncle Ty (r.i.p.) told me about my father when I was growing up...

## THE FIRST LESSON:

Big Tone, or "Bart" as they called him in the street (trust me, don't ask) was one of the best teachers, or practical professors, I've had the privilege of knowing. He was a sharp flat-footed hustler. I mean this literally, as me and my Pops share this flat-footed feature. In spite of it, however, Pops was an all-star athlete growing up, excelling at baseball and basketball. Dude even got a minor league baseball offer before he graduated high school from a MLB Triple-A ball club. Not bad for a young black man from southwest Detroit. However, the thrill was short-lived due mainly to the fact that my dad was a minor at the time – seventeen years old, to be exact – and my grandfather, John, shut down Dad's ambition like the electric company cutting the power after a missed payment. Since my dad was underage at the time, he couldn't sign a contract without parental consent. The talent scout had been watching Dad play for a while and went to great lengths to wine and dine both of my grandparents with dinners and slick talk, telling them just how badly he wanted my dad to play for the ball club. He made no guarantee that Pops would move up to the majors. However, the opportunity would've positioned him to become a better athlete, if nothing else, and he would've had a chance to do his thing on a larger scale. But, sad to say, John had other plans for my father – his stepson.

John went through the motions, went to the dinners, played the whole situation cool, all so that he could shut the whole damn thing down with a giant "hell no." Imagine my father's anger at this direct attack on his personal goal. What was my grandfather's reasoning, you might ask? First, understand my grandfather, John, wasn't really my old man's biological father; he was Dad's stepfather. That fact added kindling to the fire that burned in my dad's stomach. John was from South Carolina and had an eighth-grade formal education. He was old school and had never even learned to drive a car. So, as you might imagine, all these truths gave my father ammunition for his side of the argument. John's point, on the other hand, was that even though Dad had a high skill level and a hard work ethic, John felt his education should come first.

In my grandfather's defense, I understand his harsh perspective when dealing with my father. But reality punched Pops hard in the face during that time. Looking back, I don't think he ever bounced back from the disappointment, but more on that later. I say that to say this…despite my grandfather throwing major shade on the old man's short cut opportunity – and yes that's all it was – "Bart" still landed a full-ride baseball athletic scholarship to Southern Illinois University.

Even though that was a major upside to an otherwise fucked-up and heart-wrenching situation, my pops just couldn't let go of the obviousness of John's bullshit. While on a free-ride at college, instead of honing his skills, having fun, and enjoying new experiences in a different state away from home, instead of exploiting the situation for what it was and maybe still playing for the Triple-A club after his freshman year, or even getting good enough to go to the majors off his own muscle, my pops, in his infinite rage and resentment, pissed away his time. He partied, gambled, and stunted until he became so bored and/ or so homesick that he made up an elaborate lie that he'd been robbed in Chicago in order to come back home to Detroit. It didn't help that my grandmother was a real momma bear who loved to coddle and provide comfort to her boys.

Ever since my dad chose to cop-out and opt-out of his destiny, of what might have been, he has struggled to get ahead. I share all of this to point out that, in spite of my negative feelings about my father's decisions in life, he still contributed to my being where I am today. From his crucial life story, I came away with some significant principles and learned a few lessons.

First lesson I peeped after getting the rundown years ago was this:

In life, others will always transfer their limitations to you to make up for the inherent lack in themselves. My grandad's quick castration of my father's contract offer proved that fact all too well. Second lesson: Follow through on your potential. My dad was a badass on the court and on the baseball diamond, but as soon as a little opposition reared its ugly head, he froze and became discouraged. When the time came to switch-up and follow through, he simply got lazy and stood still.

Over the years, I've seen my pops make hundreds of thousands of dollars as a salesman and a hustler. He always kept money. This dude has never appeared broke or poor. Even when he seemed to be, it was just a game he was running always to keep people from being too nosey or in his business. I've seen him bring home 20k checks from one month of selling furniture – I even got to see him in action many times over the years. When he's focused, he's a beast in his own lane. If he wants to get money, dude can't be stopped from getting it. I realized early on that, genetically, I have the same capabilities as my Pops. It was a matter of me taking hold of the good examples he showed me and discarding the bad ones – ignoring them in order to maximize my overall potential.

For this harsh example, I thank you, Pops. You showed me a pathway to success and offered me a hard look at what life can do to a winner if he gets lazy. Because of your good example of what a bad attitude and a bad outlook can do to hinder one's grind, I breathe deeply and work harder at my dreams.

Thanks, Pops.

The above short excerpt offers a foundation and a foundational reference for readers of this motivational book. We all have had many teachers throughout our lives, and some have come from the most unlikely of sources. I've chosen to construct a pretty good play book from the game I've gathered over the years so that I can help others strive, not just survive. I want to offer you my perspective on how to go get it with Build or Destroy: A Guide to Grinding.

# BOSS BRICK NO. 1
## CONFIDENCE IS A KEY

"My attitude is that if you push me towards something that you think is a weakness, then I will turn that perceived weakness into a strength"

—Michael Jordan.

KNOWING YOURSELF IS crucial to having a winning personality. Can't nobody do you like you can, after all. If you look throughout history at famous, highly influential criminals, you'll see that, at their core, they share a form of confidence and stubbornness that allowed them to view certain situations objectively. When others would've been emotional and foolish, they knew exactly who they were at their core. If you are to be a leader, especially a great one, you must master yourself first before you can hope to master and influence another person's thinking and behavior. It's the boss that can offer a different scope that hits his or her target true over time. "M.J." is a prime example of this fact.

I won't bore you with stories about Michael Jordan's rise to fame and power; you can easily gather that information or hear the stories from relatives or friends who are fans of his legacy. I will, instead, use my outlook on him as an example to make a point.

Everyone knows Jordan was competitive; what people confuse is pinpointing his competitors. Every time he stepped on the court he was in a world of his own; he owned the situation, the tempo, and even inspired fierce energy and a heightened ability in his pseudo opponents. He only played against himself, always trying to outplay, out think, and outwork his previous performance. Jordan came into the game as a lean, high-energy, raw gem rookie. One can see this example of him in watching old playoff game film during his performance against the Celtics. Raw at the time, he focused and played off his known strengths – his youth, agility, speed, and aggressive spirit. M.J., in his early form, ran the Celtics, with the great Larry Bird, ragged. The look on their faces as the young rookie exploded to the basket, chased loose balls, and seemed never to slow down, was enough to intimidate the aging dynasty. As the seasons progressed, Jordan ran into opposition after opposition. Even teams such as my hometown's Detroit Pistons developed what would be known as "the Jordan Rules," which were specifically designed to shut "His Airness" down.

Anyone who follows sports knows that the Pistons squad was just as dominant, if not more so, when facing the Bulls in the postseason. Even before they met him in the playoffs, Jordan had the team so shook that they had to form a plan aimed at shutting him down so that they would feel better about their chances of a victory. Even then, his opponents understood what he already knew...

Jordan was the real opponent. The only true opponent. Jordan was only one man. Still, he was the leader, and he had the gift of presence with an unwavering sense of victory that was down so cold that his opponents ignored the rest of the Chicago team members. This extreme but necessary tactic worked the first time, as it helped the Pistons earn a championship – proof of the commonly-heard phrase, "What doesn't kill you, makes you stronger." Match a face to this phrase, and MJ's is the prime example.

Jordan admits that, even though the team was defeated that postseason and knocked out of the playoffs, he shouldered full responsibility for the loss, never blaming nor giving credit to the opposition. At least not in the way others in his position would have at the time. Instead, he pointed out all the shortcomings of the games, and flaws that should be rectified before the next season.

For example, he noticed that the east coast teams, mainly the Pistons, were extraordinarily physical and had a unique structure made up of large, strong enforces, drive-and-slash guards, speed, and power. On the court, Jordan could match or outmaneuver the guards and forwards and easily make his assault within the paint, splitting the defense as he did all season long. This was expected, and he pretty much had his way. That was, until he ran into those large enforcers I mentioned earlier, mainly Rick Mahorn and Bill Laimbeer, who were known for their hard fouls, trash talk, and physical presence.

Any player with the balls to go into the paint where these two hung out knew he was getting beat-up and leaving the game with bruises. The sheer physicality of the games took their toll on Jordan, who heavily relied on his strength, speed, agility, aggression, and innovation during play. After the loss, he reserved himself to the gym in the off-season to build his body up to take more physical punishment. Also, he took note of how the Pistons, and every other team, put a heavy focus on him, which limited his overall effectiveness on the court.

So, in true boss fashion, he got his team more involved. He used the focus factor to free-up his teammates, and they eventually became even better. The next season, other teams weren't dealing with only Jordan; they had to worry about the whole team plus Mr. Unstoppable himself. Jordan realized he was the center of attention and that opponents viewed him as the primary, and sometimes only, threat during a game.

Being the leader, he was, Jordan gradually became a mentor to the rest of his teammates, shouldering full responsibility for their success or failure. Ownership of every victory and every failure was one of his mantras – after all, that's what captains and real bosses do. When the following season kicked off, the NBA saw a stronger, ever more durable M.J., but with a slight, yet problematic, difference. He used his singular possession of the spotlight to naturally be everywhere at once, working his teammates at a much higher percentage than he had in previous seasons. In essence, he mastered his environment by being fearless to the point that he became his rivals' only focus of attention. Due to his confidence and his knowledge of himself and his environment, Jordan won the previous season in the playoffs, the Bulls broke down and dismantled to a hard, gritty team from Detroit, and Jordan proceeded to win the NBA championship. The rest is history.

## THE TAKE AWAY:

Passion is necessary.

Drive is a requirement.

Love for your pursuit will keep you grinding.

Time management must be studied.

Goals are the signpost on the road to success, letting you know you are moving in the right direction.

## BUILD POINT:

Confidence becomes second nature after several victories. Still, despite possessing great traits and abilities, a time will come when your steadfast gaze will fail you. Even if it was all good just a week ago, slowly you'll hit a wall so steep it seems impossible to climb. Your brilliant mind won't be able to think of an equation to help you around your biggest challenge. That's when a coach or mentor can help. Keep in mind that every master was once a gritty, hungry student.

We all possess abilities and attributes and were born with special traits. However, often it takes a mentor or coach to bring what's already within us into full maturity. Mentors challenge our norms and push us harder than we push ourselves. They know exactly how to apply proper pressure and pain for positive steady growth.

## BUILD POINT:

Remain confident. If you grind hard for what you want, keep in mind that to progress you must still be humble enough to seek help from those that have suffered and played your game at a master level. You won't regret the results brought about by a mentor or coach. The process will hurt, but no pain no gain, my brother.

Just know that, in life, you are going to suffer losses, especially when chasing greatness. It's important to remember the point of a loss or a temporary defeat is to teach you a lesson.

A true boss knows you'll often learn more from a loss than a win. After all, if you had all the answers about whatever it is you're pursuing, you'd succeed continuously then move on to the next pursuit. A loss forces you to stop temporarily, reset, rest, and reevaluate everything that went wrong. The most important thing to focus on is "why" it went wrong, rather than the fact that it did.

You must have supreme confidence in yourself so that you can give your spirit and brain a chance to work in unison to trouble-shoot errors and expose any shortcomings. By doing so, you can come back stronger than you were before. Anybody grinding for real truly knows, deep down, that they will eventually suffer losses. However, they also realize early on that maximum effort, despite a setback, only adds to their strength of resolve to come back better. Always remember while grinding that all "winners lose well, and losers, oh well."

# BOSS BRICK NO. 2
## HARD WORK BEATS TALENT

"I'm not in this world to live up to your expectations, and you're not in this world to live up to mine."

– Bruce Lee

## The Reverse Perspective (Looking at a negative/ take the positive):

REMEMBER GROWING UP and seeing this hustler, "Q," aka "Mo Scam," getting down on the streets. The hood often referred to him as Mo Scam because he was always scheming and plotting something, usually centered on getting money. What stood out to me about the guy was his uncanny way with people; you see, Mo Scam was an addict, and his drug of choice was cocaine. I mention this fact as it adds to the point I'm making.

I'm not sure just how high of an IQ level Mo Scam possessed, but I know it had to be substantial, as this dude could charm and out-debate the devil himself. Despite being intoxicated regularly, the dude had acquired a steel trap of a mind over the years, mainly due to his habit of reading books at night when he wasn't running the street on a mission.

He never went to any university of higher learning. Still, he earned an honorary degree in urban street politics with a minor in hood chemistry, which is nothing but a derivative of the modern day mainstream variety. He excelled at history, modern or ancient, which he used at his disposal when hashing out deals with the neighborhood hustlers and killers with whom he regularly consulted. If it wasn't for his drug addiction, I honestly believe Mo Scam could've run for political office. His confidence came from his years of accumulating knowledge and wisdom – his priceless education, you might say.

If a dealer was getting into the game in our neighborhood, it was only a matter of time before he had to link up with Scam, even if only for research and development purposes, or to gain vital information pertaining to current affairs in the surrounding area. Money can't buy the respect and admiration Mo Scam amassed in his life on the streets of southwest Detroit. He had to pay in blood for currency. Over time, he entered the street world and it put his life at risk. He rubbed elbows and politicked with dangerous people daily.

Mo Scam's grind is a testament to trial and error. I'd even go so far as to say he embodies the *very definition* of trial and error. His willingness to let go of self-image, never worrying about what others thought of him. His ability to learn while moving and shaking, often because he was high when he did his best work. Trust me, anyone who didn't know him would think he rehearsed every movement, fist-bump greeting, or sendoff after a job was complete. I've seen him wake up earlier than most legit working individuals and head up to one of the neighborhood car washes and wash cars from 7:00 am until well past midnight. He had his own bucket of car detailing equipment, including brushes, wax, and towels. For hours on end, he'd polish, buff, wash, and wax cars for people too lazy to do it themselves. Like any other great businessman, he fed the demand of the masses.

Various hustlers and dealers and almost anyone else willing to let him shine up their ride paid him twenty-five dollars a pop, not counting tips. He'd make anywhere from five hundred to one thousand dollars in a single day. Many of his clientele were long-time customers and proud advocates of his service.

Mo Scam didn't rely on the internet or social media 'likes' or double taps to promote, as do so many of the masses walking around today, clueless about how to carry on real business. He built his name and reputation by transforming himself into a brand on the streets. That brand came across through his work ethic and positive, fearless attitude. As I said, if he had it in him to do it, he could've gotten involved in politics as well as a legit business. But Mo Scam was a self-aware man and true to himself, stayed in his frame, and ruled his lane, proving that even a short-sighted individual can become successful when sure to purpose, and true to one's ideals.

## The Breakdown (The negative):

Often, we as flawed beings (humans), allow fear to stunt our growth and potential. To be perfectly honest, 90% of people are simply lazy. They realize early on in their grind that if they truly wanted it for themselves, they could achieve more and have virtually no ceiling for success. However, the uncertainty of what comes with success is enough to cripple most people into a mediocre life. In return, this gives them a sense of victory. In the back of their mind, tucked away nice and neat, is a case filled with secret regrets of what could've been if they'd taken the hard but necessary risks. Take from this example of Mo Scam what you will, and always keep in mind that, usually, where there's smoke, there's fire.

I believe, Mo Scam never had proper models and examples to follow in life. He allowed himself to become a victim of circumstance, and he ended up molding his grind to match his environment. While sometimes this may be necessary for survival, it'll never get you to the next level. There is no point in risking death for the sake of cheap success or dead-end pursuits. We are ultimately going to die and pass on someday, some sooner than others. The goal should be evolution and adaptation to surroundings that would crush the next person's spirits, and to use those negative aspects as positive fuel to boss-up out of the situation.

At the time of writing this guide, Mo Scam is in his late 50's. Life has blessed and graced him with almost a half a century to grind and produce something for the next generation to pick up and use to get ahead in life. Instead, his body of work is shallow. I say *shallow*, not to be confused with *empty*. I chose to observe his methods, take what I could from his experience, and boss-up with it.

Like Mo Scam, be fearless and bold in your pursuits. Best case scenario, you'll open many doors using the strength of presence alone. Just remember to grind for a higher purpose, or all your time on earth will be wasted and in vain.

## BUILD PRINCIPLE:

Be bold in your grind. Boldness gives you the appearance of a person sure of their purpose. The ability to show boldness in the face of adversity, strife, or challenge is one of the greatest weapons bestowed upon human beings by the universal God.

To a coward, boldness appears animalistic, rough, unrefined, and scary. In fact, it is all of these. Imagine watching a wolfman shapeshifting in front of your eyes into a bloodthirsty wolf-beast. Even if you choose to run away and manage to lock yourself in a secure place, deep down you still know that beast of a man is going to eat his fill of whatever prey he just so happens to come upon.

Cultivate this trait over time and realize one of the many tools of truth. Understand that death is certain, but boldness, tenacity, and stubbornness give your hustle necessary fuel to burn. If confidence is gasoline, boldness, in turn, must be dynamite – a useful tool to pull out during times you need to make a statement and get your plan off the ground. Anyone daring to stand in your way will take note of this burst of energy you emanate. The masses of haters will have no other choice but to respect how you move, so take it as a compliment. After all, handling dynamite takes balls that most people don't, and never will, have.

# BOSS BRICK NO. 3
## HUSTLE AND FLOW

"If you're going through hell, keep going."

–Winston Churchill

## BUILD PRINCIPLE:

B E ADAPTIVE. A concept that eludes the grasp of various hardworking individuals is the idea of fluidity, which is the ability to be flexible in tight binds and stressful situations. Rest assured, not taking the proper time to develop such an ability could prove fatal in the marathon of the daily grind toward success. Those that nurture and embrace flexibility can move and shake in various lanes. Flexibility provides depth and allows you to talk to anyone and see things from all angles. Without this at your disposal, you'll slowly become a stagnant body and very one-sided in your approach.

An inability to plan and be open for change will dismantle a strong idea or plan. Life is unpredictable. Allowing yourself to know this fact and having the strength to act on it are two different things.

## BUILD POINT:

You must allow yourself to adapt to things and be open to change. In this way, you can flow like water, transforming with your environment, dealing with circumstances that show up suddenly that could stop your progress if you're unprepared for sudden change. The art of adaptability is a lost one these days when it comes to hustling or grinding. I say "art" because, when properly executed, this skill is invisible to an onlooker.

Take, for example, an entrepreneur I met back in 2009 named "Germ." (R.I.P.) He got his nickname because of the way in which he chose to hustle. You see, Germ was a thief but not just any kind of thief. He stole game. For instance, if he needed to know about something to further his business knowledge or ability, he would find out who had the details then infiltrate their mind, and like a germ, pick it clean of the most crucial information.

One day we were chilling at his house in Dearborn, a suburb right outside Detroit, and Germ was smoking a joint. He always talked too much when he was high, so naturally, when he got intoxicated, I'd be right over and go into my pseudo-fly-on-the-wall mode to gather information and soak up game. Germ was a skateboarder type, and he and I met when I went to the street races near Belle Isle. He had his own skateboarding clique, his own brand of skateboards and t-shirts.

He'd always be carrying a skateboard with him and stunting on dudes with this souped-up Mustang Cobra he owned. Originally from Cali, life in Detroit for Germ was definitely a change of weather and pace. Over time, I noticed the hippy-looking dude always had a pocket full of money.

I realized right off that he had a lot of hustle about him – the way he'd spark up a convo about the cars that were about to race while passing out his business card and slowly moving the discussion to rap and hip-hop music.

A black skateboarder in 2009 wasn't that taboo, especially since artists like Lil Wayne featured skateboarding in their videos, and Lupe Fiasco's Kick Push single had already come out. Still, as unconventional as he seemed at first glance, Germ always maintained his swagger and cool around large crowds. He'd always say, "Keep up, 'lil homie," whenever he'd go off into one of his rants about music and the history of street culture as it pertained to hip-hop and fashion.

## BUILD POINT:

Know thyself. These are familiar words for most people, yet the mantra tends to fall on deaf ears more often than not, especially in this fake-is-the-new-real information age in which we now live. Strive to stay in your lane, and you'll never experience traffic jams.

Germ walked around charming people into buying t-shirts, and his cards had his YouTube information on them just in case a serious person wanted to check him out online. One thing about Detroit – we love hustlers and people who grind for their shine. Also, as always, Germ knew how to hustle and pump his product, no matter where he was or who was around him. The dope boy that was always at the races betting big saw this skinny, hipster-looking black dude mingling and rubbing elbows as if he was born and raised in the city. Germ walked up on him with his chest out, like always, and said, "Don't you hate a fucking hater?"

Dude replied, "Hell yeah, bro... nothing worse in life, my bro. Where you from?" He had a shit eating grin on his face.

Germ had overheard this dude talking about how people

in the city don't support each other right, and how the hatred was disgusting. Being the hustler, he was, Germ used this man's statement against him to further his cause. After he got the guy to admit he had a dislike for haters, Germ proceeded to tell the flashy cat all about his skateboarding brand, and that he was looking for investors to "invest and support his grind," as he put it.

The statement had a powerful effect on the dealer, due to the fact he had openly admitted being of the anti-hater variety, and all he ever did on the street was show love to anybody on their grind. The trap was set; the conversation had already infected him. He did not want to lose face in front of his many groupies and followers, so he felt forced to not only hear Germ's business pitch but to contribute or instantly become a liar in the eyes of the public.

The amount of money Germ asked for was the most outlandish part of the entire situation. "Yeah, that's right, bro!" Germ said as he demanded the funds. "I want two thousand dollars." His boldness matched the undertone of the environment. After all, demands and side bets were made at the races all night, with clever negotiation erupting back and forth between high-dollar showoff types.

The young, goofy-looking black kid from Cali had infected the foolish wannabe, and Germ made two G's in fifteen minutes simply by moving and observing his surroundings and by matching up the attitudes and energy of the situation. That, coupled with his boldness and sense of presence, allowed him to get exactly what he wanted.

## BUILD POINT:

People have various problems to deal with – weight issues, phobias of all kinds, laziness. I could go on for days about the list of kinks humans possess, but the main one is a lack of restraint.

Many people struggle with running their mouths for too long during conversations. Have you ever been discussing something with somebody and had a moment to pause and digest the information, only to have the person resume blabbering and tell you too much? Then, later, they regret telling you what they did and expect you to forget instantly everything they said?

In life, you can learn more and get more bang for your mental buck by remaining silent and observant of everything that is taking place around you, just by listening with a still mind. In life, it's important to fight for what you want if you plan on eating your share. There are multiple ways to skin a cat, and if you learn to get out of your own way, you might learn what I did long ago: It doesn't cost much to pay attention.

After many years, my friend Germ and I parted ways. Strangely enough, he joined the military in 2010. I haven't seen or spoken to him since just after 9/11. It's hard for me to picture my fast-talking hipster friend taking orders from anyone, but he was a versatile human being, to say the least. I'll forever be grateful for the conversations and boss game I received from my friend. He showed me how to have fun and get money while doing so.

# BOSS BRICK NO. 4
## ADAPTABILITY

> "Sometimes, you don't have to win, you cannot win. But that has nothing to do with losing."
>
> —Rickson Gracie

## BUILD PRINCIPLE:

ADAPT TO YOUR surroundings. In life, you will come across unfamiliar people, situations, environments, and events. We all have default strengths – the traits and abilities in us at birth. When stepping foot into an unknown level – and, yes, there are only levels – its unfamiliarity is due to the energy and attitude of the given phase. Meaning, you have to be like the late great Bruce Lee – like water, adopting water's traits, the ability to flow smoothly even through rocky environments. At the same time, water also crashes and can cause sudden damage. Water is unpredictable – still one minute, violently erratic the next. Lastly, water can run hot and transform into vapor or steam, and then be cold, forming into ice.

Point is, as is the nature of water, you must develop your abilities to exploit every opportunity presented to you. Remember, by just being as still as a calm body of water, my friend Germ was able to listen-in on conversations and key-in to critical points, becoming erratic and unpredictable, like a wave. The target became shaken by the display as Germ crashed ashore to make known his intent. But, by then, the flood was underway.

In my experience, lack of fear in any given situation is more a key to adaptation than is common sense, or even familiarity. In fact, adaptation is born out of an awareness of unfamiliarity with whatever is faced in any given moment. Anybody can pretend to fit in. We see it all the time in working environments – individuals so consumed by titles and power that they jump head first into positions they're not prepared to carry out. (But this isn't the true point.)

Let's really keep it real.

Most managers and other leaders at various companies don't have the slightest clue about the day-to-day operations of the business they supposedly oversee; they don't even know how it works. How could they? When it comes to being a "boss," information and know-how don't really matter. A willingness to step feet-first into the shit is what makes a person a leader. I frustrate many people with my view on this point.

A leader adapts to people and surroundings, manipulating matter (or people), using the skills and knowledge of others to achieve goals and get shit done. You must learn the art of letting go and knowing when to be quiet, to hear something critical to your survival.

The universe has put tools and treasure in place that will help you attain your desires. Understand that true game is never given to you – you must dig for that shit!

## THE ANT.

The ant is one of the most overlooked and underrated creatures on the planet. Humans would be more highly evolved if we paid attention to our tiny neighbors on this dirty ball, we call earth. Ants are very similar to humans. For example, most of this insect's success in so many environments can be attributed to their social organization and their ability to modify habitats, tap resources, and defend themselves. Adaptability is an all-encompassing skill that must be harnessed and nurtured throughout life.

Learn to quiet your mind, and you'll easily make room in that skull of yours to inventory more skills and knowledge. Humans are the most adaptive creatures on earth when it comes to doing and getting what we want when we really want it.

## BOSS PRINCIPLE:

Use your imagination. When the Wright bros wanted to fly, right from the start critics shot their ideas full of holes. But they knew what they wanted and would not allow themselves to be stopped by something so small as fear or uncertainty. The choice had already been made to fly; it was just a matter of finding the right people, places, and things to exploit for information, skills, and materials. Due to their boldness, the situations necessary to make their dream come true often found *them* instead of the other way around.

Working hard and grinding for grinding's sake, coupled with a lack of fear of the unknown, led the Wright brothers to innovative ideas. Over time, those ideas produced fruit that continues to benefit all of us today, every day. Learn the art of adaptation and realize that just because you aren't used to something doesn't mean it isn't necessary for growth.

# BOSS BRICK NO. 5
## STAY IN MOTION
## – FUCK THE COMMOTION

"Have patience in all things, but, first of all, with yourself"

—Saint Francis de Sales

### BUILD PRINCIPLE:

PROBLEMS EXIST TO be solved. You must realize that most of the time while you're on your grind, shit won't move or get done until you do it your damn self. Progression doesn't happen by osmosis, ya dig?! Motivated people make it happen, moving this dirty ball forward every day on their own. It's important to be aware of your doubts, but don't make the mistake of having a conversation with those doubts and fears in your mind because they will betray you every single time.

On the other hand, fear keeps you aware and awake to present danger, and doubts present themselves when the mind has its teeth into something it doesn't yet understand. Get used to being doubtful if you plan on achieving anything in this life. Please believe me when I say it's a necessary evil. Being comfortable and playing it safe is a lazy man's or woman's mantra. While striving, the feeling of uncertainty, fear, and frustration act as signposts on your road to success, giving you a different kind of vision.

Common phrases often uttered about patience by individuals without the slightest clue of the true definition include: "Take your time," "Patience is a virtue," and my favorite, "It's a marathon, not a sprint." These statements reveal no real experience by the speaker when it comes to the practice of working and waiting for an opening or opportunity to present itself.

Truth is, most people miss entirely the countless chances available to further themselves over their lifetime. They fool themselves into thinking they can wing-it and work without a plan in place. Living such a lifestyle is like putting a key into your car's ignition, starting it up, then hitting the gas with the car in park. Imagine carrying out this same scenario every day for years. Seems pretty silly, huh? Well, that's what a person looks like when grinding without a purpose, just idling high while the days pass by.

Often in life, you might come across people you'd label as opportunists. You know … the dude waiting for you to slip up with your girlfriend or wife so he can swoop in like fucking Cupid and put a fake facade love bullet into her skull. Unlike what most individuals might think, in some cases that guy or girl isn't wrong to do that, or an asshole. He or she simply works and waits like a tree-top sniper for an opening to arise, and then takes a shot.

This code of patience holds true for any style of grinding you choose to use on your journey to success and happiness. Everything worthwhile takes time, effort, will, skill, and a high level of tenacity. All these traits contribute to the grand scheme of things, yet time is a must-have ingredient.

## NATURAL LAW: THE SHARK

Some sharks must constantly swim to keep oxygen-rich water flowing over their gills, but others can pass water through their respiratory system by a pumping motion of their pharynx that allows them to rest on the seafloor and still breathe. However, sharks do have to swim to avoid sinking to the bottom of the water column. The ability to move up and down freely in the water column is, in fact, one of the extraordinary adaptations of sharks.

## BUILD POINT:

Even in nature, motion is emphasized as it applies to the baseline survival of many species. Be sure to thoroughly contemplate this fact.

# BOSS BRICK NO. 6
## YOU'LL NEED EVOLUTION BEFORE REVOLUTION

"Big difference between grinding slow…and not doing shit"

—The Builder

## BOSS-UP OBSERVATION: The Snail.

IT'S EASY TO pass judgment on the snail and call it slow because we move past it so quickly that it appears to be sitting still. We forget that the snail is forever in motion.

While working for anything of worth, there will come a cost, and most of the time you'll have to pay in blood. I do not mean this literally, but as a way of explaining that the universe can be a harsh taskmaster, especially when it comes to teaching necessary lessons before a blessing is handed over.

Bossing-up is more than just a phrase; it's a way of life. Don't get life twisted. Often, while on the road to success one tends to face all sorts of issues and problems that put roadblocks in the path ahead. Keep in mind that rough patches such as these are there to test your strength and resolve. They are life-filtering mechanisms meant to weed out the undeserving and the unprepared.

---

"You can do whatever you want, just figure it out"

—John free

---

My grandad John, a.k.a. Mr. Free, always gave me bread crumbs of game whenever he saw me scratching my head, trying to figure out my next move on this chessboard of life. Despite all his stubborn faults – and, by the way, we all have them – he is a very rich man with a wealth of experience. No schools were close by where he grew up, and he came from a family of farmers who owned land, so John only had an 8th-grade education. The family did a lot of manual labor, and after reaching a certain age, the children were expected to help make a living.

I remember my grandfather telling me how grateful I should be that I have multiple pairs of shoes to wear. When he was coming up in the south, he and his many siblings didn't even have shoes, as the family didn't have the means to afford them. And they had no vehicle, so walking everywhere was simply a way of life.

Living in such circumstances made my grandfather a very innovative, durable, and creative man, as he had to maximize any opportunity afforded to him daily. He realized very early on that, even though his life was full of drawbacks, plenty of avenues for self-improvement and skill-building existed.

Because he grew up in the rural south and so deep in the country that his nearest neighbor lived at least four to six miles down the road, you might imagine just how far he had to walk to get to the nearest store, market, hospital, or police department. If something broke around the house, John and his brothers or cousins had to fix it. If they didn't know how, they had to figure it out. Doing so in a crunch taught John about patience and critical thinking.

My grandfather has never received any formal training as an electrician, yet he has rewired entire homes, as well as replaced plumbing, renovated bathrooms, and built porches. As a child, waiting for a repairman or carpenter was just not an option.

Also, since he lived outside of the city limits in an area surrounded by thick forest, he developed an affinity for nature and an appreciation for life. Fishing for hours on end added to his training in the art of patience. Plenty of sleepless nights went by when the fish refused to bite and offer my granddad a victory. Through this experience, he learned what it was to be told "no" and gained an appreciation for the word. John said it added to his joy when success finally did arrive after much hard work and, of course, persistence. He always said to me, "The success train is never late for the man that's early to the station waiting for it to show up; it's always on time."

## BUILD POINT:

You'll always feel broke and poor if you never take advantage of the good at your disposal.

Often, time is our only advantage. If one is blessed to have it, time is a significant teacher. Evolution and growth require a certain level of patience and wisdom. It also helps to be told 'no' a few times in life.

Growth has a hidden tax that goes along with its often-expensive price. That tax is in the form of pain, stress, discomfort, and pressure. There is a reason some people say that only a fool refuse to change. Change is inevitable and certain. With each day that goes by, you're growing older; you simply can't help it. Time waits for no man in this world; it simply keeps moving, whether you like it or not. So, it's best to make friends with time and use its resources wisely while you're able-bodied and can do so. After all, nobody wants to hear an adult complaining or crying all the time — only children and the elderly reserve that right.

# BOSS BRICK NO. 7
## LIKE A BIRD OF PREY

"People only see what they are prepared to see."

—Ralph Waldo Emerson

**BUILD PRINCIPLE:**

GRIND WITH A clear intention. There's a lesson to be learned from all that takes place day-to-day. Remember, everything relates to everything. Like the snail, we, as hardworking dream chasers, must learn from and use all to which we're exposed in this life. From our perspective, the snail moves at a slow pace, but from the snail's point of view, it is moving at its max speed based on circumstance, environment, obstacles, predators and, lastly, its desires. The fact that it moves slowly isn't a fact at all because its frozen movement is a matter of outside perspective.

The snail is only slow to you and me. It grinds hard to cross the street, to make it home and eat its next meal, to keep from being eaten itself by an enemy, as is the natural order of things.

However we might look at it, the snail knows the truth – that all of the aforementioned can happen. It knows this truth instinctively and accepts its fate should it meet with any of those scenarios.

The snail could, of course, succeed in its pursuits or fail miserably. Still, despite its inability for speediness and its lack of coordination, it continues to move with the intent of going wherever it wants to go and getting there. The fear of destruction isn't even an afterthought — the snail grinds for grinding's sake.

## BUILD PRINCIPLE:

Be persistent in all pursuits. Like John and the snail, we must learn how to persevere despite our past, current, or future life situations. Learning how to turn base metal into gold or make sugar from shit, as my gramps would say, is an essential element of the human growth experience. We are the alchemist of our existence; seriously ponder that fact. Remember that everything you're going through can make you or break you. That's the nature of this game we play.

Some people are born gifted with more tools and easier living conditions than others. Still, as I continue to stress, even that is a matter of perspective. Take note: due to depression, even monetarily rich people often commit suicide. To many people, that fact seems silly and unfathomable; however, a person's life isn't always as it appears to be.

My grandfather grew up poor as hell, "just keeping it real." Still, he and many others from similar starting lines in life have made it their business to run their race to the best of their abilities, as we all should. And at the end of the day, keep it skull-noted that steady persistence coupled with an unwillingness to accept any situation at face value has and will ultimately lead to success. After all, it's not the landing or the takeoff that makes a flight memorable. It's the time spent sitting, interacting with the people to the front, back, left and right of us while basking in God's glory, all the while looking out our small but clear window and developing an appreciation for the is-ness of all things.

Because of his strong examples and the many breadcrumbs my O.G. dropped at my feet, I learned gratitude for my food (experiences), and it's because of it that I eat hearty meals and live abundantly.

Thanks, Grandad, for the love and all the game.

# BOSS BRICK NO. 8
## WILL OVER SKILL

"Exercise is done against one's wishes and maintained only because the alternative is worse"

—George A Sheehan

## BUILD PRINCIPLE:

THE REFLECTIVE GRIND state: People I've met on my journey often tend to want a lot out of life. But as many of you reading this book know damn well, wanting something and wanting it badly enough to go after it are two different cadences.

I've had my share of lazy days. Just know that the day you tell yourself what you need to do, and your lower-self debates that encourage you to the point of submitting and taking it easy is the day you'll regret have negative self-talk. We all have them, and that brings me to my next point. Willpower is one of the most powerful forces you can summon while on your respective grind.

Muhammad Ali is famous for saying how much he hated, not *disliked*, but absolutely *hated* training. However, he understood early on in his career that he'd be facing stronger, faster, younger and, at some point, hungrier opposition.

As many of you know from history, Ali used his tremendous willpower to fight against the notion of getting drafted and going to war. He was labeled a radical because of his bold, outspoken behavior. He truly had a brass set of balls to go against the government at the height of the civil rights movement and the many other social issues going on in our country during that time in history. Ali was an all-around fighter, not just within the squared circle but also in real life.

The Great One knew, deep down, that his skill set wouldn't be enough even though he possessed a beautiful setup jab and excellent reflexes. He knew that in order to be a success, he would have to draw on a force unknown to the losers – a.k.a, the haters of the world. That force is the treasure of willpower. Ali fought many opponents that exemplify how he used the tool of willpower. The one I choose to focus upon is unlikely to some, but I'll use Ali himself as the example.

Any man that can get into so many fighter's minds, as he did, had to be self-aware and self-conscious about his own short-comings. To be a professional boxer or a professional anything, you have to possess the discipline to work toward reaching a certain level of craft, to tap the ability of foresight of getting through those grueling training days and throwing thousands of jabs and the miles and miles of road work it takes to raise cardio to that of fighting condition.

In many ways, the daily grind of life reflects and is like this training, if you're trying to be great at anything, that is. You must realize, as Ali did, that every second is a gift to be treasured and honored by putting in maximum effort in all your endeavors. Reflection on one's current flaws and limits can provide insight into how lazy you might be. After all, flaws don't exist unless they are debilitating in some way from an uncontrollable genetic defect. So, as a fully capable human being, you must realize that you genuinely have no flaws or limits holding you back from what you want. The bottom line is, even though we are born with infinite imagination, we hobble our ambitions most of the time due to our lack of honesty.

Self-reflection is a necessary ability you must integrate into your psyche until it becomes natural to do so. Only then will you be able, like the great champion Muhammad Ali, to defeat your true and only opponent – yourself.

# BOSS BRICK NO. 9
## DEEP ROOTED

"Patience can cook a stone."

—African proverb

## BUILD PRINCIPLE:

B E THE ICEBERG. When training your mind to overcome conditioned behavior caused by society, pop culture, and family traditions, it's important to remember your candle's slow burn of success. Understand this and understand me: nothing occurs overnight. When was the last time you planted a seed, and after twenty-four hours, a giant fruit tree sprouted up out of nowhere?

During our respective life journeys, I'm certain we've all come across individuals who convey a winning spirit. Everything these people touch seems to turn to gold over time. This type of person has a unique flair for things many struggle to understand, such as how to build productive relationships with people and how to have an air of confidence beyond the usual puffed-up variety. A certain heaviness is in their aura when they step into any room that seems to say, "Yeah, I have this shit figured out." Scary part is that most of the time they do have a lot figured out about this part of the game.

I have come to view the success model of these people as the iceberg stage of the grind. This stage is tough to attain, frankly, because it takes a combining of the principles mentioned above and examples of reaching the grind's heights or, I should say, its depths. The iceberg level is often a felt kind of energy that successful beings possess. This level is earned through will, patience, a cultivating of useful stubbornness and, finally, an acceptance of one's mortality.

When you're on your purpose, grind, or whatever you choose to call it, nobody is going to check for you and keep track of your progress. If anything, your failures will be taken down and cataloged by your enemies, frenemies, and haters. Like an iceberg, your real power, resilience, patience, grit, and passion will never receive appreciation from those on the outside looking in. Therefore, success must start and end with you; others are too busy complaining, bitching, and feeling down about the very life they're choosing to live daily to ever really give you a second look.

If anything, many people will hate you for hunting down your happiness. The point is to know your depths and attune to the nature of things, what you bring to the table, and the heaviness of your work ethic. Having this profound sense of knowing will give you the inner strength to withstand any insult or slight from those with the same repetitive, routine views of society at large.

I knew an entrepreneur named Rick that I called "R-Smooth" because he was always working on a plan. Just when it seemed as if he was slowing up or falling off, he'd surprise those around him with another grand display of success from his hustle. I met him when I went to Atlanta for an entrepreneur workshop. At the time, I was working for an airline, so I got free flight benefits. I'd always fly out to go to my apartment in Houston, or I'd find an interesting chance to learn about business in a roundabout way. He knew right away that I was from Detroit, just by my fit and demeanor. Many Detroit natives travel or move to Atlanta, among other places.

R-Smooth got into a heated debate with me about my thoughts concerning the traditional college approach to knowledge, and I guess we finally hit a stalemate. I explained that I wanted to be my own boss, and he was already doing that himself. You see, Rick's grandmother left him some money in her will, and he flipped it into real estate and a car detailing business. You could say he was lucky, but it took the dude at least five years to see any real money after his initial investment.

After I heard his story, we agreed that he would consult with me on matters of real estate and his formula of success, although he was only five years older than me. For two years after that, I flew to Atlanta every three months to chill, listen to R-Smooth's teachings, and take notes. Whenever we'd kick it and cruise around in his S500 Mercedes, Rick would say to me, "Bro, patience is one of the hardest things for people in this life to master." After a long pause, he added, "I received over 200k after taxes from my grandmother."

During the time we spent together in Atlanta, he was twenty-eight and surrounded by temptation in the form of fast women, drugs, and other thrills of life. Instead of spending a dime of the money he'd inherited right away, he meditated for a year. "Going in an instant from a couple of thousand in a bank account to over 200k is a scary feeling to a person without a plan. Or at least it should be, Bro!" he'd say to me.

His decision to fall back and think was his saving grace. He was able to back up and look at the situation objectively, choosing to put emphasis and focus on both his strengths and his weaknesses. He spent a small percentage of the money on real estate classes and received his Realtor's license then researched forming an LLC and a corporation.

Rick devoted at least forty hours a week to reading any book or article he found on the internet about entrepreneurship and business ownership. He spent almost every minute of the day planning and revamping his moves and training his mind to be more patient by enduring events and situations that normally would cause anger and frustration in a person. These situations included taking the long way home after work and going down streets that had notorious long traffic lights. When he would dine out and a baby or child made loud outbursts in the restaurant, rather than getting disturbed, he would practice embracing the noise and accepting it.

This strange training, he put himself through helped prepare his mind for business. Because of it, he became a millionaire at age thirty-one, just two years after he received that money from his deceased loved one. Of course, he invested his inheritance in various ways to gain additional wealth. Still, the main take away for me from this period in my life was his stillness and relaxed demeanor when it came to handle more at his disposal than he had ever before possessed.

I've learned many things during my short, yet fruitful, existence. Still, I'll never forget the value gained in realizing that I don't really know anything. A person can gain immense power by just going inward and discovering what limitations, vices, and potential self-harming behaviors might be lying in wait for them, especially after experiencing a windfall.

You should heavily contemplate this concept as you boss-up.

## BUILD PRINCIPLE:

Be patient and passionate. Like Rick, sometimes we receive immediate opportunities that allow us to skip levels in life. This can be both a blessing and a curse, and for many it's often a curse. I say this because, without realizing and admitting right away that you're unprepared for a big jump, you might not slow down enough to gather the proper skills and resources to benefit you after entering that new arena. Patience is one of the many tools in this game you must cultivate and work hard to master, or at least gain a healthy level of self-control over. Grinding off sheer impulse will most certainly lead you down a path to failure, mainly because you'll be rushing your harvest.

The seed of success must be planted firmly in the back of your mind; plan your every move like a coded treasure map. Only you know the final digging spot, but you also are aware of the obstacles and tools necessary to gain access to your prize. It's never enough to want something; that's how children tend to think, and nobody wants to hear you cry about how badly you want something in life. We are all after our definition of happiness; just know that true grinding comes at a price. Time waits for no man, so learn to work while you wait. When the smoke clears and you're standing tall, despite what a hater might say, they'll have no reason to debate.

Imagine that you buy your dream car, whatever make and model that might be. Picture walking into a car lot and telling the dealer exactly what you want, from the color, body, interior – everything. Now, see yourself pulling out of the lot and taking a long drive home. See all your family and friends waving and smiling at you, shouting out how proud they are of you. You feel good, and the new car smell is so intoxicating. After some time, cruising around, you finally make it home.

Now, imagine stepping out of the car and slowly making your way into your lavish home. Enter the house and make a right into the living room, then proceed to stare out the wide glass window at your dream car sitting in the driveway. This next step might be hard for some, still it's necessary for this exercise to work properly.

- Picture yourself staring at the car for the rest of the day.

- Then go upstairs and go to sleep.

- The following day when you wake up, go downstairs and stare out the window again at your dream car in the driveway. Make yourself something to eat, get dressed, and walk outside.

- Detail your car until it's so clean, so beautiful.

- Now, after you finish cleaning your well-crafted machine, after all the hard work you put into it, make a vow never to drive and enjoy the vehicle again.

Crazy exercise, huh? What's even crazier is the number of people subliminally doing this very sort of thing within their everyday lives.

## BUILD POINT:

It's always wise to make do with all lessons given. Realization is a beautiful thing that leads to self-mastery. There is no point in self-sabotage; it leads nowhere worthwhile.

The next time you're thinking about sinking your teeth into something new, ask yourself if you want the new thing bad enough to suffer a little while smiling a lot.

I know that many of you are reading this saying, 'Damn, that's a stupid thing to do.' I admit that, yes, it's foolish, considering how hard you must work to be able to pay cash upfront for whatever it is that you want. Not to mention all the time, pain, and discipline it took for you to produce and save the money.

Truth is, the stupidity that we all agree is on display in the new car exercise should give you insight on how silly you look every time you pursue anything half-heartedly. You might produce good ideas and thoughts, but they're nothing more than a fantasy fabricated within your mind unless you take the necessary steps to make your dream happen. The car you want, the dream house, the admiration and love from your peers, is only in your mind, and that's a good start. However, just seeing it won't make it tangible. You must also make all the moves necessary to allow the image to grow.

Every piece of fruit you've produced during your lifetime was premeditated; you must understand this deeply. Some individuals are so malnourished when it comes to being fulfilled successfully that they'll literally take whatever they can get. They allow a defeatist mentality to creep into their psyche that produces inevitable suffering over losses. Rest assured, this will happen. But you must remain conscious of the truth: Wins and losses are illusions and temporary; they can't be held forever and must be let go. You must move on from them once the valuable lesson is learned.

## BUILD POINT:

Like a mighty tree that stands tall in the middle of a rain forest, you need to maintain your footing on your path. Understand that growth comes with all sorts of challenges – some large, some small. Reach for the sky (like the tree) and constantly fight gravity, even when your arms grow tired.

Maintain good soil; a.k.a., your inner circle, your family, and your team. In this way, your growth will be constant, despite what the weather of life brings your way. You'll remember that you're a strong tree that started as a weak, fragile seed. Stay deep-rooted; you might sway and move, but you'll never break and fall over.

## THE INTERLUDE:

The grind is my ritual, while my smile remains invisible.

And, no, it's never enough. Cold-hearted male ambition the size of a blue whale, thoughts too heavy to weigh on any scale, refusing to fall asleep…I'll never become a sheep. A lone wolf with a chipped tooth.

Smart enough to know that ignorance is bliss.

Still, I love the truth.

Chillin' with demons from my past at my dinner table.

They're always feasting, unconcerned, as my hunger goes deeper.

So, I'm always beast-in.

I have been a friend with my dark side for so long that I despise the light. Wrestling with my family, I pull away with all my might.

Because I love the fight.

Ran away from love more times than I remember.

Rather remain a frost giant…screaming as I uproot trees.

No need to yell "timber."

Family tried to starve me out instead of supporting my dreams.

I vowed to escape by any means.

Went from soft and loving, to hard and hateful.

I discovered a new inner strength, and for that, I'm grateful.

And, yes, I realize how all this can seem depressing. Still, this is my journey, not yours, so no need for the stressing.

This pain I have remains heavy on my chest, but that's why

I grew strong in the first place. So, like the bench, I'm going to keep pressing.

## THE INTERLUDE ...

# BOSS BRICK NO. 10
## ASK THE HARD QUESTIONS

---

"If you're complaining, you're focusing on the wrong damn thing – the builder. I'm not waiting for shit, especially my money!"

—Worm (R.I.P.)

---

"**M**AN, MY MOTHER is a dope fiend, and my pops is doing life in prison," my friend Worm would tell me when I would see him at the park.

I would hang with my homeboys at the park on the weekends when I didn't go over to my grandparents' house on the southwest side. Worm was fifteen, but dude was sharp as a razor when it came to sales and marketing campaigns.

I noticed how Worm would always serve people dime bags of weed in between our basketball games at the park. He stayed fresh every day; new Jordans, gold chain, and a gold plain-Jane Rolex, all at age fifteen. I know what you might be thinking; typical drug dealer, street thug. Well, my friend was far from typical. He was a straight-A student, honor roll, first one to class each day and last to leave. I'd purposely bomb a test and get a B simply because I didn't care for perception at that point in my life. We'd head to the Coney Island on 6 Mile and Schaefer after test days to chill for a minute, and he'd always call me out.

"Yo, Ant. Why did you answer the test questions wrong on purpose?" he would ask me; these situations happened often.

"Well, because I can, Bro," I'd answer boldly with my arrogant undertone.

"That's our problem, Bro," he'd say. This was the moment when I knew he was just as ambitious as I was. However, his hindsight was very clear at that point. He went on to say, "I make straight A's and walk a straight line and talk clearly to everyone I meet because perception says, 'Here's a young man on his purpose, on his job, and about his business.' So, I get respect and extras because I go above and beyond."

Of course, I had to jab back at his neck. "What extras?" I asked with a sarcastic grin on my face. "You're slaving away and going through the same bullshit as the rest of us."

Worm's face went blank as he stared through the dirty window at the Coney and out into the moving traffic. After a long pause followed by a deep breath, he went on to explain, "I get extras such as extra credit assignments that I can bank along with my regular grades. So, the two to three days I'm absent because I'm getting my hustle on … they never affect my grades or attendance records. They've never had a negative reflection on my grades, my brother. Furthermore, I've already paid for my grade up front by investing my resources, ya dig? Not to mention, I'm such a laid back, mild-mannered kid. I can do no wrong, at least in the eyes of the faculty. Or so the simpleminded adults think."

After a long pause, he continued, "I managed to find out the teachers' likes and dislikes, and even some of their vices, such as alcohol for some and weed for others. I help maintain their vices by supplying them with things in plain sight, whereas before they'd have to sneak and be deceptive to get what they wanted. It's because of these business transactions that I receive extras, my bro."

As young as Worm was, he already understood one of the most important rules of business.

"Ant, you always got to know your market if you want to do good biz, my bro," he'd tell me after making a sale on our walks home from school. To be honest, my brother was a prodigy at that business dealing method. I admired the guy very much during those times, not for what he did, but because of his motor for success and his ability to maximize his surrounding resources.

Unfortunately, however, my friend's race to the top was short-lived. Life in Detroit isn't always sweet as pie. In fact, it's more often bitter. My friend Worm was murdered the next summer — by whom, I don't know. But I still remember the bit of advice he gave me the last time we chopped it up and talked.

"Realize how big you are before others try to put cuffs on your mind and your grind."

Worm was a fifteen-year-old boy, but he had the mind of a wise man. I'm forever grateful that our paths crossed when they did. R.I.P., my brother.

A POEM: DEEP WITHIN.

Ode to my friend,

Too cold to hold close to the skin...

My only comfort is these heavy hands

pouring out pain thru this pen or my favorite pencil.

Lord knows if everyone could appreciate what I stencil.

My ink runs deep within these veins.

Or, should I say, genetic caves or an ancient ruin.

Dare to delve deep into my mind...

lean forward and smell what I'm brewing,

quickly pulling back frostbitten fingertips

as you shook my hand. A hard heart I possess,

as a result of my stress.

Stuck at society's mercy...no shield...no vest!

Chest cavity twice removed to replace the Freon,

I'm chilling...an emotional villain.

If I could exchange all the hearts I've stolen for cash...

I swear I'd be making a killing...

it's not my fault beautiful...

after all, you were willing.

Soft legs spread...east and west. Eyes like rockets...

ready to blast thru the ceiling.

Deep within, I remain ice cold...

after me, the mold remains broken.

Fearful my overall design was too bold.

No-pain-just-all-gain is the motto of the fearless.

It's a blessing and a curse to have vision so peerless.

## BUILD POINT:

The goal should be to go legit one day. I've met plenty of highly-skilled young men and women with a knack for business, hustling and making it happen – plenty of dope boys with fortune 500 brains and a street mentality. Often during the journey, ambitious men and women get stuck in their own way.

Point is, change is a good thing, and seeking its mystery by stepping off the cliff of uncertainty shows growth and fearlessness. I'm not here to tell you what to do; I'm only a true friend, unafraid to let you know that being one-sided, narrow-minded, and stubborn leads to a quick death, or a long miserable one. Above all, remember that only a fool rejects change.

Are you wise, or a fool?

# BOSS BRICK NO. 11
## DON'T TONE DOWN YOUR VOICE

"Never apologize for what you feel. It's like saying 'sorry' for being real."

—'Lil Wayne

**BUILD POINT:**

YOU MUST MAXIMIZE the full potential of your surroundings, your environment, and the people on the chess board of your life. You could move through life and make plenty of enemies. If you pursue righteous aims, expect to be met with plenty of opposition.

There is no such thing as a positive or negative situation. Reality is a painting of your own creation, and the paintbrush of fate is forever fixed to your palm. What are you painting? If you one day wake up to chaos, it is your fault and your doing.

You'll never hear a successful, happy, or fulfilled individual say, "I never did shit. All I did was sleep and never took any risks or learned the business of dealing with people. This shit just happened one day." Like the painter, you must pay attention to each stroke of your brush. Paint what you want to see, and I guarantee that when you take a step back, you'll see the beauty of your effort and patience.

## BUILD POINT:

Once you figure it out, you'll be unstoppable.

Example... Bossed-up Dreamer: "Hey, we been cutting hair since high school, right?"

Dream Killer: "Yeah! Why?"

Bossed-up Dreamer: "We should go set up a meeting with homeboy from down the street that cuts hair, and we can get a couple of other barbers together, too. Together with him, we could build a business inside of two years just from sharing a clientele base."

Dream Killer: "How are we going to do that? You're thinking too big, my man!"

Bossed-up Dreamer: "That's why we'll succeed. We have a plan we need to stick to it and see through to the end."

I remember having this same sort of conversation with my so-called friends at the time. I surrounded myself with 'how-and-I-don't-know' kind of people. I could blame my young age or the fact that I grew up in Detroit, could easily make up a story about how the crime and drama of the street outside my door somehow prevented me from thinking straight and remaining focused. Often, we weigh ourselves down; we sleep on ourselves, our skills, our gifts, and, sadly, our lives overall.

We oppress ourselves by buying into the negative movie of life or "society's dream." Understand that this planet that the universal God created for us is huge. It's meant to be seen, traveled, studied, and admired. It is dangerous to launch your dream or purpose out into the world. It means a new way of thinking, a new mode of operation, innovation, and the clearing away of the status quo. A lot of comfortable conformists will fight to keep you quiet, stop your hustle, and kill your ambition. For these old dinosaur day-to-day thinkers, your dream means destruction! It means warfare.

## BUILD POINT:

You have all the weapons and resources around you to carry out your battle plan – your purpose.

Every encounter you have in life will either help you or hurt you greatly. If you plan on winning, surround yourself with individuals and teammates that enhance your grind, and stay away from those throwing salt in your direction.

# BOSS BRICK NO. 12
## THE CHESS MATCH

> "It's life in every breath you take…and that's dope
> as fuck!"
>
> —The Builder

L IVING IN AMERICA is crazy, especially in this new-age era, and
it can be extremely overwhelming to the body's senses. We
live in an ugly, yet beautiful, time. In this country, we can
pig out on a pizza while watching a "reality show" that displays
extremes of obesity. We gorge ourselves and shake our heads at
this fat person on the verge of death and immediately feel better
about our life situation, as it were.

We have technology that makes our daily lives super easy. For
example, you want to know at what temperature saliva freezes?
Search for the answer using your $700 to $1,000 cell phone.
Maybe you want to know how to make a seafood casserole you've
seen on the Food Channel, so you search for the recipe, and there
you go. The method might even include a video link of a real chef

cooking the food while giving specific instructions with do's and don'ts.

After a glorious internet search session, we can cook said meal, and before we take our first bite, take a picture of our efforts and post it online for the world to see and praise our chef skills.

We have a delusional view of the world at large, as we live in our self-made hell. We have so much at our disposal, yet we always focus on the next thing that we don't yet possess. We are desensitized to small, yet very important, things in our lives. It's funny that the simple things do the job and work to our benefit and betterment, yet they're invisible to the naked eye. You must feel them, and what's understood doesn't have to be explained.

## BUILD POINT:

You'll never change anything about the world by trying to be anything like it.

Originality is a rare thing to come by these days. Sad part about it, nobody seems to see it that way. Make sure you use your eyes and see the world for what it is – it isn't all rose-colored glasses.

# BOSS BRICK NO. 13
## IN CASE SHIT HAPPENS

"Let us rise up and be thankful, for if we didn't learn a lot today, at least we learned a little."

—Gautama Buddha

**BUILD POINT:**

IT'S EASY FOR humans in all of our awesomeness (so we've been told) to neglect the powerful, yet simple, driving forces in our lives.

Breathing, for example, is often taken for granted hourly, by the minute, and down to the second. Gratitude is what the raw hustlers on the street tend to understand. Work hard, bust your ass, fall, then get your ass up for some more.

This is, of course, the romantic part of the grind. However, showing gratitude for being able-bodied enough even to pursue your goals in the first place (whatever they may be) should always remain in the front of your mind — having this simple acknowledgment of "being" will act as a performance enhancer for anything you choose to accomplish on your journey.

Cool thing about this drug "Gratitude": it works 100% of the time you use it, and the side effects are beneficial. Side effects include:

- focus during tough times /react-text

- ability to smile at fear /react-text

- ability to pull strength from similar goals you crushed

- ability to step back to get the full picture of what you're trying to paint with "your hands."

In case some shit happens:

- Keep your weapons (Grind) loaded.

- Train your soldiers. (Get and keep a strong team.)

- Pick your battles. (Fight for tangible, achievable things based on your current situation.)

- Make allies. (Get a mentor that can help you see the fight or terrain from all angles.)

- Keep building. (Keep fighting for your dream.)

- Defense is what keeps you in the game.

In the end, the defensive mode wins the game. You don't have to win by blowing out your competition. One point is all it takes to win. Remember, "your only opponent is self."

What do I mean?

Everyone has an organic self – the real you that God made that is untainted by domestic programming, that is capable of greatness and blessed with world-changing abilities. This self is fearless, loving, giving and ambitious. Still, there's another person inside, one born out of fear, pain, uncertainty, and hate forced on us by society, television programming, family, friends, and those who would label you a useless eater.

This coward that dwells inside our minds is a powerful parasite, and he's been in the hater gym all day, every day. This negative figure is strong as fuck, but only when we neglect ourselves. If you're going to block a shot and keep someone from scoring, stop the fearful side of yourself and laugh at it. You need to pursue your goals with a full heart and unshakeable intent.

## "The Mentality" poem:

Take special care of every step I place on the ground.

The world looks upon me with, the same deadly frown.

The same frozen stare that seems to lock my senses.

I'm blind, deaf, untouched and tasteless.

I can't put my finger exactly on what's there; I can't feel what I see.

Nor can I hear what my mouth wants to say.

I'd just be crippled, and beaten, beyond repair.

The world stands over me like a bully,

looks at me in pain as I struggle to pick myself up

from the beating I just received

from the hands of a war-torn world.

Asking myself, who are we to become angry?

The world only knows destruction and carnage; that's all it can inflict!

## BUILD POINT:

Understand...it's not the fastest, the strongest, or the most feared that succeeds. It's often the calm, the relaxed planner who looks ahead and factors in all possible outcomes before the first move is ever made.

This is chess after all.

# BOSS BRICK NO. 14
## WHO ARE YOU?

"He who knows others is wise; he who knows himself is enlightened."

—Lao Tzu

**BUILD POINT:**

THIS GAME WE play is not always offense based. It takes defense to take those profits and invest in real estate, the stock market, startups, so that your hard-earned money naturally appreciates over time, and then it works equally as hard for you.

It's a great blessing when we recognize our strengths early on in life because you can lean on them to help you get ahead and run up the score. However, you better make sure you're continually working or refining your weaknesses; otherwise, you'll do yourself a terrible disservice.

> "What happens if you die? Well, your babies are shit outta luck, homeboy!"
>
> —The Builder

So far, I've spoken encouraging words of wisdom and offered a few examples of how to move and shake through this game we call life. However, I'd feel very foolish if I didn't make sure we touched on the bitters of life, also, when it comes to talking or discussing "the long walk," "the long night" a.k.a. death, or transformation, as I like to view it. Very few have the stomach to deal with the stimulating but painful truth of reality.

From the time of our birth, the hourglass of life begins to pour out. Crazy part is, no one knows how much sand (time) they were granted by the universal creator. Did you know that at the time of writing this book, most modern American millionaires, about eighty percent, are first-generation millionaires? Usually, the fortune they build will dissipate by the second or third generation. However, one upside to this fact is that the average millionaire goes bankrupt at least 3.5 times.

Now, I know you're probably saying, "Just how in the fuck is going bankrupt a good thing?"

Simply put, it shows evidence of an individual's unwillingness to give up, not to mention the obvious hustle, ambition, and charisma of their character. After all, it takes a lot to become financially well off, and suddenly you end up falling off. Losing all of your money at least three times over might seem insane, but only a focused person can see the light despite the overwhelming darkness of the moment.

This brings me to my next point – life insurance. Remember, I'm not an expert; I like to make sense and play the game how it's supposed to be played.

**BUILD POINT:**

Play the game like it's supposed to be played or get played yourself.

One way to create a first-generation millionaire in your family is by leaving your children a nice head start on life, at least in the form of significant financial investment on the part of their late parent. How many seemingly perfectly healthy humans perish daily from sudden cancer, car accidents, wars, or simply taking a left turn down the wrong city street?

I don't know about anyone else, but I don't want my picture on a t-shirt while my family argues over how to bury or cremate me. Not to mention my spouse and children are left destitute, at least for the time being. Not to say your significant other won't hold it down if your clock suddenly gets punched. But a million-dollar insurance policy is relatively cheap. Depending on your health and age, you can set up a thirty-year, million-dollar policy for around $70 a month. This amount is like your daily membership at a gym, fitness center, or martial arts dojo, for all my warrior readers. That's $840 a year, which is more than worth it to me to be able to leave my wife and son a million dollars.

How cool is it to teach your son or daughter all you know – how to invest, grind, and love life? At the same time, knowing in the back of your mind you've made a life investment early on that will bear ripe, tangible fruit. To all my focused few reading this, I'd like to pose a question: What could you do with a million dollars, knowing what you know now?

**BUILD POINT:**

There's more than one way to invest; remember, you're playing chess, not checkers.

Life insurance is one of those things never taught to people, especially African Americans and other minorities, and is not taught to youth, either. This could be because of the significant reality of a lack of respect for us as human beings.

The perspective on things ...

At the time of writing this book these are statistics on Number of deaths and leading causes of death in 2017:

- Heart disease: 633,842

- Cancer: 595,930

- Chronic lower respiratory diseases: 155,041

- Accidents (unintentional injuries): 146,571

- Stroke (cerebrovascular diseases): 140,323

- Alzheimer's disease: 110,561

- Diabetes: 79,535

- Influenza and Pneumonia: 57,062

- Nephritis, nephrotic syndrome, and nephrosis: 49,959

- Intentional self-harm (suicide): 44,193

The examples on the previous chart provide a flash of reality for many people. Death is the only authentic guarantee we have in this limited life of ours.

I've been nothing but honest so far, so why act nice about reality all of a sudden? For instance, I've used Jordan himself earlier in this book as an excellent example of what real perseverance, laser focus, and grinding from a place of inferiority looks like. However, I now must use the Jordan brand as another raw example.

Americans have a great number of priority issues when it comes to taking care of themselves and their families. To get shit done, we must admit our shortcomings. The Jordan brand, for example, has captivated millions of Americans for the better part of 25 years. That's roughly a quarter of a century of the masses spending their hard-earned U.S. dollars on a fictitious piece of fashion apparel, and all in the name of promoting a status symbol.

We've been hypnotized into worshiping symbols of power, success, and wealth, instead of grinding for real power, becoming successful, or building wealth for the present and future generations to come. For instance, take the average price range of a Jordan shoe. Depending on the rarity or popularity of the model, the price might be anywhere from $100 to $500 or more.

Now, let's say, for the sake of arguing – though this fact is hard to argue – that the system hypnotized your parents, either as a result of being fans of the game of basketball or "MJ." Let's say that they decided against their better judgment to purchase these status symbols for you from your infant years through your high school days. Being modest, of course, let's say Nike released four pairs of this particular shoe each year, and your parents bought you two of the four pairs each year. The breakdown of cost could be reflected to look something like the following:

Two pair of Jays at an estimated price point of $130 a pair equals $260 a year. If you multiply this amount by eighteen years, this equals $4,680.

Remember, some parents do buy Jays for their children from the time of birth. Note that this is a modest example; this doesn't include inflated prices, nor does it include any other merchandise purchase, such as matching caps, jerseys, and other clothing. The point I'm trying to stress is that even being modest, the average amount spent could be a minimum of five grand.

Let's take a look at Amazon.com, Inc., which is an American

electronic commerce and cloud computing company that was founded on July 5, 1994 by Jeff Bezos and is based in Seattle, Washington. In 2017, the current stock price was trading around $1,000 a share. Now, let's go back ten years to the year 2007 to see that the stock price was trading at a high of $94.45 a share to a low of $37.87 per share from December 2007 through November 2008.

Let's say that you took that modest $4,680 spent on Jordans and bought shares of this company when it was at a low of $37.87 per share. You could've roughly bought 123 shares with it. Also, let's say you held those shares for ten years. You and your loved ones would currently have $123,000 from making a small investment. Now imagine if you invested consistently over those ten years.

You see what I'm saying yet?

A saving grace, despite all of this, has a tremendous amount to do with the "knowing" part. You should be fearless as a result of the wisdom to which you've been exposed within these pages. Always strive to invest heavily and early in your children, because anything can happen to you.

The last thing you want is to be the dead-beat father or husband that didn't think ahead and hold down the fort, even from the grave. I've overstated what I'm stressing to you in this chapter, my friends, because it's just that simple, and at the same time, just that serious.

# BOSS BRICK NO. 15
## IDOLS ARE RIVALS

"The thermometer of success is merely the jealousy
of the malcontents."

—Salvador Dali

MANY SO-CALLED "WOKE" or conscious African Americans refer to the black men in their lives as "king" as a term of endearment, respect, and encouragement, but with no extensive connection to or education about black royalty here in the Western world. I say that to say this: If you feel, know, and think like a king, you will frequently have opposition come in and out of your life.

People have this notion of, "Oh, I'm qualified, I'm superior," or "I'm the shit, I should be in this position." That, my friend, is all well and good, but along with that innate intuition or knowing comes a chilling vibration that others can feel, smell, and see when you walk into a room.

If you allow it, lesser humans will do any and everything in their limited power to destroy you or pigeonhole you at a lower standard in the world.

Historically, kings and queens are powerful, charismatic, diplomatic, and, last but not least, fearless in every endeavor they pursue. That's what makes them a king or queen in the first place. It's the reason your homeboy makes a joke right to your face when you share that enormous dream you have. His fickle, subordinate mind cannot allow his dormant conscious mind even to digest the possibility of your dreams taking place, because that would mean he must get off his ass and get into motion or be left behind when you get a foothold on your ambitions.

Wars have been fought throughout history, and for the most part, the causes are the same. One ruler feels intimidated by a more assertive, loved, bossed-up king in a neighboring land. Naturally, this mad king is threatened, not because he is lesser in any way, but because of his inability to focus on his own kingdom and success. He can't help but compare his kingdom with another.

One of the major keys to self-mastery, or what I often refer to as bossing-up, is developing your inner selfishness. I know some of you might be saying right now, "What?" Well, simply put, inner selfishness translates to *one who is unaffected by lesser beings' demands or restrictive mindsets and philosophies.*

As ambitious people with big dreams and goals, we must learn not to give a fuck what the lesser humans think, feel, and believe daily. I say this not to sound harsh or rude toward the existence of others, but as an observation about what it takes to move forward on your journey to success.

## BUILD POINT:

Some individuals reading this will say, "This same ol' bullshit – he's not telling me anything I don't already know."

I suggest you go back and revisit this book's previous pages to gain more clarity before you continue reading. Knowing something – or "of a particular something" – is one thing. However, knowing how all that shit ties together is a whole other ball of wax.

Take "haters," for instance. By definition, a hater is a person who simply cannot be happy for another person's success. Rather than be happy, they make a point of exposing a flaw in the successful person. Hating, the result of being a hater, is not exactly due to jealousy. The hater doesn't want to be the person he or she hates; instead, the hater wants to knock someone else's hustle.

This basic definition speaks volumes in terms of the human spirit and its role in the warfare of mankind. Furthermore, it's not as much about the so-called hater being unhappy because of the happiness of another.

It's more the admiration of an equal and the need to dominate a rival-type of philosophy. People you deem to be haters, or at least who appear to be, are usually students of your example. It's because of this observation that I believe that no person walking this earth can honestly say he or she has never hated another human being. Especially in the United States where it's competitive 24/7, our system grooms and molds people to jock for position, strive, thrive, and out-do God. That last bit might seem a bit overblown, but if you grew up in the U.S., you know full-well that modern-day North American theme.

Here's a news flash: No matter whom you dislike or who doesn't like you, the price of tea in China is not affected. Ya dig? Point being, instead of wasting precious energy thinking about the fact that your success is making the next person salty, take every insult, nasty look, and complement with a grain of salt and season up your grind.

## PERSPECTIVE:

"What goes up will come down" is a familiar phrase we often hear in life. This simple law of physics directly applies to our daily grind; however, many on their journey through life have lost this law. Understand that, although you might have dreams that could be life-changing if brought to fruition, that doesn't guarantee that along the way, the mission won't suffer the usual ebb and flow.

Learn to appreciate any opposition you face. Usually, it's the universe testing you, as all things require checks and balances. Without them, anyone could get whatever they desired by simply sitting idle and asking for it to show up.

Ponder this fact thoroughly and, boss up.

# BOSS BRICK NO. 16
## IGNORANCE IS BLISS

"Let the past stay dead; after all, if you woke up today, you're alive now."

—The Builder

'M SURE IF you're still with me on this journey, you might have cursed me, laughed, or had your feelings hurt a little. Well, guess what! The world doesn't give a shit, and that's why I'm writing this guide to coach and motivate you through the bullshit our shallow world conditions us to accept.

At the time of my writing this book, we are living in the "information age," an age in which you can gain insight and information on nearly every subject known to man, all from a handheld computer or "smartphone," as the masses call it. Never before in human history have, we been so informed and at the same time so misguided.

I know you're saying, "Here we go with another rant, and how does this apply to grinding, success, ownership, and business?"

I'm merely trying to paint the base layer of this canvas of thought for your mind to digest. I have a question: Why is it easy to learn multiple languages, martial arts, or anything else when a child, but difficult when you become a full-grown adult?

Well, to sound technical, kids learn faster than adults because adults have a more developed prefrontal cortex of the brain, which stores working memory. Due to the development of the prefrontal cortex, adults experience functional fixedness, and that makes adults see everything exactly as it is.

A child's more simplistic mind can out learn, out know, and outdo any adult's because they are ignorant of their ignorance. As adults, we learn at a faster rate, but our previous golden sponge has been tarnished and clogged with abuse, conditioning, entertainment, and social media bullshit.

By the time we hit our mid-teen years, our retention ability has been sliced and diced to the point of being nonexistent. The average human being's attention span has been reduced to the level of a zombie. Most current statistics say that the average attention span is down from twelve seconds in the year 2000 to eight seconds now. That is less than the nine-second attention span of your average goldfish.

## BUILD POINT:

To achieve anything you seek, you must nurture and hone your attention and, secondly, remain comfortable with the notion of being ignorant.

Why do you think ignorance is bliss? I don't mean in the sense of ignorance as it pertains to a lack of knowledge, which is, in most cases usually not viewed as a good thing. (However, certain situations exist in which you are happier not knowing the truth.) I mean ignorance in the sense of your relentless pursuit of learning about anything unfamiliar, unburdened by fear due to a childlike curiosity.

Children are fearless, aren't they? Which is why parents must keep a sharp eye on children so that they don't break the veil of curiosity too much and kill themselves during the process of self-discovery. Ignorance is truly blissful, my friends, until you bump your head trying to run head-first through a brick wall. Then, due to your curiosity, you learn one of the laws of physics without ever reading a single book on the subject.

Remain ignorant of everything and, at the end of the day, you truly know nothing. By being honest in this way, you leave yourself open for new discovery and allow your natural evolution to take place.

# BOSS BRICK NO. 17
## THE MIRROR

"It is much easier to show compassion to animals. They are never wicked."

—Haile Selassie

"The secret of life is to have no fear; it's the only way to function."

—Stokely Carmichael

S O FAR DURING this conversation, I've touched on various subjects and offered insight on how one can use lessons from unsavory events to achieve levels of success in life, as well as in business. Still, despite the nuggets of game and examples I've dropped at your feet, I must touch on a subject a lot are aware of, yet very few attempts to master in their lifetimes. The lesson is 'fear.'

I refer to fear as a lesson for various reasons, one being that it's a required class we must pass if we're to transcend to new heights not yet touched. First things first. Let's get a basic understanding of this overstated bullshit term.

Fear is an unpleasant emotion caused by the belief that someone or something is dangerous, likely to cause pain, or a threat. Let's break it down.

First off, I described it as an "unpleasant emotion." An emotion is "a natural instinctive state of mind deriving from one's circumstances, mood, or relationships with others." Most of the time we allow our circumstances to direct our moves too much as we navigate the waterways of our lives. We hear these statements all the time in the hood… "My mom was on drugs." "My dad was locked up." "We were poor growing up, and we lived in the hood." "I wasn't hugged enough growing up." The list goes on.

I care about you enough to be honest with you, and I'm here to tell you that just because you were too young at one point in life to have any real power to change your circumstances doesn't permit you to play victim once you grow older and able to strive and do for yourself.

Life's not about what happens to you, especially when you had no real say so at the time of your birth of what would take place. It's entirely about what you do when the ball is in your court; you better get an understanding of that fact.

The next definition of 'fear' I mentioned is 'dangerous,' the belief that someone or something can or likely to cause you or a loved one harm or injury, that a situation is likely to cause problems or to have adverse consequences. To develop a successful mindset out here in this cold world we live in you're going to must get used to dealing with a healthy dose of adversity. Make friends with it; it'll be one of the best friends you'll ever have the privilege to meet.

I know some are reading my words and saying to themselves, "He sounds crazy as hell right now. Who in their right mind accepts difficulties and misfortune?" The answer is simple, my friends. Bosses accept it! Those with a willingness to suffer, bleed, naturally overcome, and succeed while being put under a microscope and blamed for everything…be it good or bad. Here are some brief examples of this philosophy acting itself out in real life:

- She is one of the most successful and wealthiest people in the world today, but she didn't always have it so easy. This woman grew up in Milwaukee, Wisconsin, and her cousin, an uncle, and a family friend repeatedly molested her. Eventually, she ran away from home, and at age fourteen she gave birth to a baby boy who died shortly after. Her tragic childhood didn't stop her from becoming a force. She excelled as an honor student in high school and won an oratory contest which secured her a full scholarship to college. Now this bossed-up entrepreneur and personality has the admiration of millions and a net worth of $2.9 billion. She is Oprah Winfrey.

- After vacationing in Canada, this man developed polio, which eventually left him paralyzed from the waist down for the rest of his life. Even though he couldn't walk, he went on to lead the country as one of the most respected and memorable presidents in U.S. history. He was former United States President Franklin Roosevelt.

- This pursuit of happiness author once spent a night in a train station bathroom and had a childhood marked by poverty, domestic violence, alcoholism, sexual abuse, and family illiteracy. He now has a net worth of 60 million dollars. He is Chris Gardner

- This rapper and actor grew up with a teenage mother in Queens, New York. He often recalls his mother's drug use, which fueled his early rap lyrics. His mother died when he was eight years old. He began hustling and briefly allowed his unexpected circumstances to manipulate his talents until nine bullet wounds helped him hit a vital reset button on his life. He used his pain and passion for success to fuel his animal ambition into a lucrative music career which then translated into branding. He inked a deal for the sale of his premium vitamin water for a reported $60 million to $100 million. After filing for bankruptcy, this personality used the setback to prime him for a major comeback. He finessed his way into film and now has one of the highest rated shows, aptly named "Power." At the time of this writing, this individual has a current net worth of $155 million. Of course, I'm referring to Mr. Curtis "50 Cent" Jackson.

## BUILD POINT:

You must understand that fear is an illusion, a highly-rated television show that the masses tune into daily. This doesn't mean you have to go the way of the do-do bird. Like the examples of success stories I gave you, you must be willing to accept the slings and arrows of the universe if and when they launch in your direction. One thing that separates the sheltered and privileged from those that have to go through more than their share of bullshit is that the ones with scars and wounds have a more realistic tale to tell before they die.

More importantly than the scars and pain, they are far more equipped to handle anything life throws at them. For example, during the 2008 recession, more than 10,000 recession-related deaths occurred in the United States alone. Many of these premature deaths were well-off, well-established, tax-paying people. Despite how financially well-off they thought they were, they made a critical mistake. These people thought the universe and the government gave a damn about them. They had no idea how to overcome or persevere because they had always played it safe, never taking any risks or suffering hard hits or setbacks like most of us do.

Just imagine going from eating sirloin steak every week and golfing every weekend, to eating Top Ramen and working two jobs just to pay the utility bills. Many high-minded Americans could not bear to deal with such a brutal reality. At the end of the day, they couldn't face that person in the smoky mirror and know, deep down, they weren't going to boss-up out of that bullshit.

What about you?

"The Mirror." (A poem.)

The road less traveled,

The bullshit doesn't matter.

The bullies will be thrown to the four winds,

As my beamer wheels spin… eyes shifty with times.

Crafty with my rhymes… originality, what a sinful crime…

if there is such a thing!

Best believe I'm a king… with my hands full;

Sifting thru boss moves, I swear…

You gotta grind until you see the grooves.

Bones scream for more brutality...

In this, the silent quest, this metaphysical protest:

"Can melt this iceberg attached to the wounds in my chest."

Throw away your urge to thrill,

Focus on what's real and ripe for the taking.

Harvest your hard work.

Become sharper and lighter in spirit.

Walk down each goal, never give chase.

Manifesting takes time and takes its toll.

Crossing bridges…then we burn them down,

the smell of charred remains of the hating trolls.

The only opponent is self. Just remember when you climb the ladder slowly, everything eventually becomes top shelf.

—Anthony R. Barber, Jr.

## BUILD POINT:

Learn to get out of your way and stay out. We often can and will become our own worst nightmare if we allow ourselves to live in a land of make-believe. Face your fears and remember that you are your only opponent.

# BOSS BRICK NO. 18
## CHANGE –VS- TRANSFORMATION

"Let me just say peace to you, if you're willing to fight for it."

—Fred Hampton

WHEN YOU EXCEL and grind for what you want, you're going to feel pain unlike anything you've ever experienced before. This holds true for many things in life; it is my observation that everything relates to everything else in some way, shape, or form – just depends on your vantage point. Let's take a look at a person known as an "addict," meaning he or she devotes or surrenders himself or herself to something habitually or obsessively.

What is the difference between a meth, cocaine, or heroin addict, and a hustle, sports, or musical addict? Well, one could make the argument that the drug-addicted person destroys himself and, slowly over a period, kills his family as well as all his other intimate relationships.

Drug addicts develop a devotion and surrender to the habit

of smoking, snorting, or injecting that shit into their body day in, day out, thus becoming obsessed to the point that their every breath, thought, and heartbeat focuses on the next high. Does this sound about right?

Still, if we dive deep into this subject, we must ask a simple question: How is that any different from the forty-plus-year-old sports addict father who knows more about a professional athlete's life on and off the court or field, than his own child's wants, needs, interests, hobbies, likes, dislikes, and feelings? How about the so-called happily-married wife who, despite having the man of her dreams, beautiful children, and a home that's big enough to shelter three families, somehow feels inadequate compared to the celebrities she sees in music videos and on reality television shows, not to mention the seemingly perfect internet models constantly on display?

This woman is addicted to chasing a false sense of perfection. She needs a bigger ass, smoother tits, fuller lips, foxtail eyelashes, and all the other fake bullshit. Over the course of days, months, and years of obsessing over the false, she loses her grip on her already-perfect existence. To her, what she's thinking, and pursuing is still valid and legitimate. However, when it comes to anyone she's close to – those on the outside looking in – she is an obsessive-compulsive addict.

Let's dive even deeper now…

Empty your mind, be formless, shapeless — like water. When you put water in a cup; it becomes the cup. You put water into a bottle; it becomes the bottle. You put it in a teapot; it becomes the teapot.

---

"Water can flow, or it can crash."

—Bruce Lee

---

## BUILD POINT:

Obsession is a great thing when harnessed correctly and aimed at a tangible goal. Otherwise, it is like starting a fight inside an empty room. (FYI: They stick people like this inside of empty rooms...remember that.)

Addiction, simply put (in my objective outlook), describes a temporary scratching of the surface of human perfection and adaptation much like Bruce Lee's water example, along with the beauty of attempting the process in the first place. Before you shake your head, let me explain.

The process of addiction shows and proves just how powerful the human mind and will are when aimed at a definitive target. What makes the experience toxic to the person chasing his or her high is an inability to harness and control one's appetite for the desired result. And it's mainly because that result remains undefined. With no goal laid out, the pursuit is feeble, like chasing after the wind. A crack addict who is never satisfied is no different than a championship-level athlete who has tasted the nirvana of the sport for which he or she has trained and competed in for years.

## BUILD POINT:

This book isn't for the unrealistic or for those that suffer from "diabetes of the brain." (Those that only prefer the sweet sugars of life and never accept the bitters.)

If you never bother to evolve and transform over time into the butterfly, you'll grow bitter, empty, unfulfilled and trapped in the larvae stage of life. This is how obsession and addictions are born...from a sense of lack along with an emptiness of the spirit.

For example, society will label gang members as "low lives." However, these collective people will sacrifice and die for other members of their gang. They do not hesitate to support one another. They love it when the entire gang is on "top." They're all about show and prove they have fire and determination that can't be bought or taught at some seminar. They truly focus on what's in front of them, and the growth of the moment. No time for bullshit!

Meanwhile, so-called high-minded individuals are inherently divided. Everyone wants to be better than everyone else that is sharing their space. They forget that it's lonely at the mountain top and that life ebbs and flows. Meaning that, eventually, they'll grow stagnant and lazy on that mountain. As they look out across the valley, from that vantage point, they'll see mountains taller and even more beautiful than the ones they have already conquered. Or so they thought.

As with all things, they must humble themselves and begin a descent down the mountain (pseudo success) to start another journey across the rough, dangerous terrain of life until they reach another peak, all so that they can become humbled once again. The difference between the ignorant and the know-it-all is that one stays stagnant and eventually becomes older, bitter, and hateful. The latter remains ignorant, but by doing so, grows and becomes more blissful.

Change -vs- transformation.

## BUILD POINT:

We are all one, and it is important that we keep this truth close to our chest.

If you're good at something, what's the harm in teaching someone who doesn't know how to do what you do, or doesn't understand the concept? If you are good at what you do, at being you and doing you, how can sharing the knowledge be a threat to you?

Unity is a word often wasted more than the word love, and it only has weight through action. Without action, unity is just talk. Even a baby can do more than love. Love, too, only has weight through action. Otherwise, it's just talk. Like I said, even a baby can do that shit!

# BOSS BRICK NO. 19
## TAP IN OR TAP OUT

"Faith is the silent partner/investor to everyone's success."

—Tha Builder

FAITH IS OFTEN a fragile subject. I say this because out of all the various animals, creatures, and heavenly beings occupying this dimension, it's the human being that can have the wind knocked out of their sails, often daily. More lowly creatures never struggle with this issue throughout their life, growth, and death cycle.

For instance, the phrase "only the strongest survive" is a flawed humanistic phrase. Nature uses us so-called higher-minded beings as an example of how to move and shake through life. Nature will teach you how to survive, and if you look closely enough, it'll school you on how to thrive in life as well.

## BUILD POINT:

In the wilds of life, many variables must be understood, studied, practiced, and sharpened to a fine edge through discipline, focus, and passion.

What does this have to do with faith? Well, for starters, in the jungle size doesn't make you king – ask the elephant. In every room, individuals with strong egos and a hefty vibrato are afforded temporary respect amongst the rest of the animal community. However, being the biggest, or appearing as such, is no guarantee you won't be tried and tested. That's why you'll often see these ego-driven types moving in packs that are like-minded.

Usually, if an elephant-type individual in his or her prime goes unchecked they can easily take over their surroundings, the sickly or younger types are more susceptible to being taken down by the more predatory types. These ego driven beasts might keep growing until they take up all the space in their relative surroundings.

Having access to your ego can be a good thing when you need to block out influences from other people temporarily. This energy will afford you a certain stubbornness for clearing away things that impede your freedom of movement on your road to success.

## BUILD POINT:

Above all things, when dealing with accessing your ego use a healthy level of caution and respect for the destruction it can bring you.

Being large can be useful but, unchecked, can quickly turn you into a target for those who get off on taking down big shots. Humility is key to balancing your ego, so strive to attain balance as you boss-up. Hunters of the bold have none.

Size most certainly makes you a threat to some and a force

to be reckoned with, at least when it comes to the ego's energy. However, the fact remains that a big ego will never let you rule, and if you do, you most certainly won't do so for an extended period of time. When it comes to sustaining your presence and peace of mind during this crazy ride, it's the lion that reigns supreme when compared to its counterparts.

We hear all the time that "only the strong survive," and "survival of the fittest," as well as, "fight or flight," and the sayings keep going. What do these quotes have in common? They all speak to the spirit of survival, reminding the feebleminded to keep their head above troubled waters.

These phrases are for the weak-minded and weak-hearted. What's the point of keeping your head above water if the strong currents are carrying you to a waterfall at the end of the raging river and ferocious crocodiles occupy the deadly waters below? I don't know about you and yours, but I'm more of a "find a way out of the damn river before I'm thrown over and killed" kind of guy.

There's a reason the one percent is referred to as the "one percent" by the other ninety-nine percent. First place is exactly what they focus on in life. Fuck your feelings. Are feelings contributing to the end goal and positive results? The answer is no, and just as the saying goes… "next."

The happiest, most awe-inspiring people that walk the surface of our tiny planet have developed an innate ability to block out bullshit once they realize it no longer serves them in the relative and positive energy flow of the present. As I stated previously, a person with an overblown ego and a large elephant have much in common. Both are powerful and have an ease of pace and a sureness, at least on the surface. This being the case, the opposite of this animal example would have to be the lion, or its more popular title: king of the jungle.

The lion is considered king, but why? Before I go more in-depth on this comparison, allow me to give you an example of how nature codes everything perfectly and how it directly relates to the human experience. People with an exuberant ego have most likely been feeding this beast for years, especially if it's to the point of being uncontrollable to the person wielding it.

Being ego driven, you'll always feel like you are anxious, over-alert, and on your toes. After all, an elephant is so large that it must always remain on its toes, so to speak. The body of the elephant (or one's ego) can grow to such a large size that it, over time, becomes impossible to even sleep in a lying-down position; it lives life forever on its feet.

People blinded by their passions could easily make a statement such as, "I'd rather die on my feet than live on my knees." While this statement might hold significance for some, it doesn't address the main issue at hand. Since lying prone in the wild with such a massive frame doesn't afford a beast the swiftness or reaction time necessary to defend itself or flee the scene, the elephant's only security relies heavily on the ability to keep standing tall until they fall dead, even if rest is what's needed the most. (The same is true of the ego-driven person.)

Being overgrown makes an elephant or (someone with a large ego) easy prey for a fast-moving, quick-thinking predator or person. If your sole purpose is simply a focus on being large, you'll end up like an anxious, easily spooked elephant – doomed to focus on the peripherals of life, never able to concentrate and appreciate what's directly in front of you.

## BUILD POINT:

I suggest you strive to become the rider or, better yet, the trainer of your inner elephant (ego).

Learn to use your ego's power of stubbornness to clear the field of useless debris – people with defeatist mentalities, negative thinkers, and the unmotivated. When you need some extra resolve and confidence to keep moving, even when you don't feel like it, tap into your ego, but only when it serves you.

After all, if the ego didn't hold any significance, why would it exist?

# BOSS BRICK NO. 20
## THE ONLY OPPONENT IS SELF

"Great ambition is the passion of a great character. Those endowed with it may perform very good or very bad acts. All depends on the principles which direct them."

—Napoleon Bonaparte

HUMANS ARE THE only creatures, at least from my limited understanding of the universe, that make a glorious mess of things surrounding them. The reason for this guide is to give you, the reader, a little perspective on how everything directly relates to everything else in one way or another.

Further perspective will show very simply how animals respond to their environment at any given time. Humans, on the other hand, primarily react to things, people, and events. The animal kingdom respects the elephant, but that doesn't stop a pride of lions from testing the elephant's chin.

I'm using various animal examples to show you how humans are, indeed, like other living beings. Learn to tap into the truth, which is a realization that life is finite – it won't last forever. The process is ever-changing, from moment to moment, minute by minute, down to the second.

Animals are hardwired to live life in a certain way, mainly due to an ingrained ignorance. Humans are structured similarly; however, we can choose to forgo our ignorance (free will), try to fit more and more frugal information into our brains if we'd like, although most of it is useless and trivial at best. To grow, hunt, survive, and thrive, animals in the wild focus on what they learn from birth and the immediate environment in which they live.

A lion is born knowing it's a lion and is trained only in the ways of the lion. What would be the point of trying to teach a lion cub how to fly if it doesn't have wings? In fact, it has no notion of what wings look like or feel like.

I say all this simply to express my perspective. Humans can recreate using the earth as raw material. We can use metal for a frame, sand to make glass for a windshield, animal skin to make leather, cotton to make seat padding, all the way down to fine-tuning the inner workings of an engine or electrical system. It's amazing that all the electrical and mechanical devices mankind has crafted resemble the inner workings of a human being and the outward appearance of various animals. It took two brothers and various others to invest in a collective imagination to recreate flight like that of a bird in the wild.

We have created vehicles with the speed of the hare and endurance of the tortoise to move through our daily lives. We are not God and, no, we don't know everything. However, as a group, we know much more than we do alone, and together we can manufacture anything our vivid imaginations can cook up.

Somebody that hustles and grinds understands sacrifice, balance, patience, and the concept of ebb and flow. Nature automatically bestows this ability by default to the autopilot creatures that roam this planet alongside us. Be kind to nature, as you should be kind to yourself.

## BUILD POINT:

Allow yourself time to make mistakes, fail, and fight for what you want. Get comfortable with the notion of maintaining a childlike ignorance in all things.

During the return to ignorance phase, your stubborn preconditioned mind and body will resist this change. You'll find yourself no longer worrying about the trivial matters that do not serve you or your best interest.

Like a free bird in the wild, you'll develop an ability to seek freedom and fly wherever you like when the opportunity affords. For example, notice an ant's ability to shoulder large amounts of weight and to use and build team concepts with close "friends, family" and form "business relationships." Understand that you cannot build and form a solid structure by using sand as a foundation.

## BUILD POINT:

If you aren't sure about what you want to be or what your life purpose or works will be, that fact must first be okay with you.

I encourage you all to jump into life. What do I mean? You can never know exactly your strengths and weaknesses if you never attempt to learn and develop as wide a variety of skills and abilities as possible. Doing this, you will develop a healthy respect for nature and the patient cycle of life. Over time, you'll see that life is never all bad or all good; it's just right!

## BUILD POINT:

Boss-up over your own bullshit.

Behavior is said to be self-sabotaging when it creates problems and interferes with long-standing goals. The most common self-sabotaging behaviors are procrastination, self-medication with drugs or alcohol, comfort eating, and forms of self-injury such as cutting. These acts may seem helpful in the moment, but they ultimately undermine us, especially when we engage in them repeatedly.

Vices are a part of human nature. However, unchecked, even fun recreational activities can become dangerous and slowly evolve into a burden. These are limiters, created by crafty, lazy individuals hell-bent on killing off original human thought, recreation, and the developmental process. It's all you and your thoughts that dictate the outcome of your efforts or lack thereof.

I'll leave you with a perfect example of what an overzealous approach toward life will get you in the end. Let's talk about the fall of what might have been. Here's a quote from the former undisputed and undefeated heavyweight boxing champion "Iron" Mike Tyson:

"On January 8, 1990, I got on board a plane to fly to Tokyo, kicking and screaming. I didn't want to fight; all I was interested in then was partying and fucking women." And so, begins Mike Tyson's recollections of one of the most famous upsets in the history of the sport.

"I didn't consider Buster Douglas much of a challenge," remembers Tyson.

"I didn't even bother watching any of his fights on video. I had easily beaten everybody who had knocked him out."

These quotes from the former champ speak volumes to Tyson's

behavior and his principles at the time of this significant turning point in his decorated career. As I mentioned earlier, a behavior is said to be self-sabotaging when it creates problems and interferes with long-standing goals. This statement would be a signpost in the champ's career for years to come.

The champ also stated that his opponent, Buster Douglas, was "not worth sweating for," while Tyson was spending twilight hours in Japan sweating out plenty of effort and stamina with the local Japanese girls. "Besides having sex with the maids, I was seeing this young Japanese girl who I had sex with the last time I was in Japan." Robin, his wife at the time, "would go out shopping and I would go downstairs to the back of the hotel where this young girl had a room. So that was my training for Douglas."

With the fans of the sport now older and wiser, they can step back and look at this example I'm laying out objectively with a critical eye. Why is one of the most dominant fighters in history looked at more as a novelty rather than with reverence? This same champion known for knocking out men, breaking jaws, and dropping the most intimidating ring walk in boxing history during a sparring session with Greg Page. Page gave Tyson such a runaround that Don King had to drag Tyson out of the ring after a single round of sparring, King angrily shooing the paying public out of the gym.

Tyson also arrived in Japan thirty pounds overweight and made a bet with Don King that he'd make his fighting weight on time. Despite heavy drinking, partying, and constant leg-wearing sex, he arrived at a slim 220 pounds. To add insult to injury, Tyson also is quoted as saying the day before the fight, "I also had two maids at the same time, and then two more girls, one at a time, the night before the fight."

The concept of "your only opponent is self" speaks to the individual operating from a place of pure self-ownership and a willingness to run his or her life as if it's their business, which it is. The champ arrived in Japan early, not to train hard and to focus his mind on his opposition, but to party and treat the trip like a joke. He was correct in his thinking, but his viewpoint was in reverse.

Douglas trained the hardest he'd ever had to in his entire career for this one bout. He arrived in Japan all business and focused on his meal. In comparison, Tyson was so unconcerned with being prepared that even his corner men and trainers followed his example. By the end of the fifth round, his left eye was in bad shape, closed shut. He went back to his corner to discover that his team hadn't bothered to bring an ice pack or any end-swell to relieve the pain and reduce the swelling on his eye. Being as carefree as the champ, they used a latex glove that "looked like an extra-large condom filled with ice water."

Everyone knows that Tyson was like a rabid dog in the ring, fighting off pure instinct in the eighth round when he managed to land his signature uppercut to land a knockdown. History is written about this fight more than I care to remember. Still, it's a prime example of what can and will happen to any individual who forgets that to have his meal, even a lion has to work just as hard as any other animal in the kingdom. The lion, like many other animals in the kingdom, always owns his duty and position with a full heart.

That's what bossing-up is all about — self-mastery, self-discipline, and self-ownership. At the very end of each day here on earth, it's you and that foggy mirror staring right back at you. It'll expose your flaws, and it's up to you to accept and improve them or go crazy arguing with a vague reflection.

# BOSS BRICK NO. 21
## DON'T GET READY, STAY READY

"Give me six hours to chop down a tree, and I will spend the first four sharpening the axe."

—Abraham Lincoln

## BUILD POINT:

S TUDYING AND SELF-IMPROVEMENT is like good sex – blissful, relaxing, and creative while being lazy and complaining resembles masturbation – fun temporarily, awkward, a waste of creative juices (no pun intended).

Recent studies have shown that at least thirty-three percent of Americans have no financial plans, and no strategy or forethought put into place to offset those sure-to-arrive rainy days. Two out of five Americans (forty-three percent, give or take) haven't "spoken to anyone," friends or family included, about retirement planning or being their own boss, according to the studies. What's more interesting is that twenty-one percent of Americans are "not at all confident" that they will be able to reach their financial goals.

How can you even hit any goals if you never start in the first place?

I've come across many individuals with sound financial goals and various strategies and methods for turning thoughts into things. One thing they all have in common is the very fact that they're mostly young individuals in the so-called black community.

## CURRENT DILEMMA:

The trouble with being black in America (at least as it pertains to modern day living) isn't the color of our skin. Not anymore. Facts show it has to do a lot more with us as a people and our wanting to stay behind as the rest of the world moves in a progressively forward-thinking way.

I know this is about the time in the book where my more self-righteous brothers and sisters chime in an attempt to burn it. Before you get ass hurt by my objective viewpoint, allow me to paint a picture of perspective so you can understand just what I'm trying to say to your right and left brain.

## BRIEF HISTORICAL FACTS:

Slavery happened, and it was the most horrific, brutal, bloody, and unproperly documented atrocity in modern American history. People were treated and sold like cattle at the local market. Original names were stripped and replaced by a foreigner's surname. Families were torn apart, our women raped and abused. The men were lynched, castrated, and brutalized for merely existing.

## ADDITIONAL FACTS:

One can no longer be killed in the United States for trying to expand your mind or learn anything. Of course, I'm referring to the simple act of reading. "The action or skill of reading written or printed matter silently or aloud." Frustration comes to the forefront because, despite being able to freely seek knowledge today on any subject or skill we care to learn, we choose to cultivate and master frivolous bullshit.

Instead of nurturing things that will benefit us, this fact is treated as something humorous. We are, indeed, the laughing stock domestically and on an international level when it comes to the progression, advancement, or evolution of a people.

## ENHANCED SMARTS:

As I explained in previous chapters, animals are born hard-wired by genes that have not been tampered with for hundreds or thousands of years. Filling your unlimited human brain with mind-expanding information frequently would feed the imagination of a simple-minded, lopsided, task-oriented slave and turn him or her into an otherwise free-thinking being.

## READING REDUCES STRESS:

I understand why people were stressed-out daily when they were able to hurt each other openly. It would've been great to dive into a book to escape reality, or perhaps to study a book on black-smithing. Could have used the knowledge to fabricate blades and keys to unlock our chains, exposing the lie of captivity.

## GREATER TRANQUILITY:

Reading, learning, and traveling via the imagination regulates and helps stabilize the reader's heart rate. A good book with useful, practical information provides the equivalent of a calm movie we sneak off to watch and daydream, to escape from the nightmare of an otherwise cruel reality.

## IMPROVED ANALYTICAL THINKING:

A critical component of visual thinking gave us the ability to solve problems quickly and effectively. It involves and provides a methodical step-by-step approach to thinking that, if used, would've allowed us to break down complex issues into single and manageable components. Our imaginations would've been under our full control, not a slave master's.

## INCREASED VOCABULARY:

If you had been a slave, increasing your vocabulary would've easily helped you express or state clearly what you sought and desired. Vocabulary provides an ability to understand the meaning of something. Only a child can make the excuse of, "I only hear what you say, never what you mean." As an adult, you must learn the difference between the meaning and purpose of something. You would've never bought into the notion of "master and slave."

Eloquence is another skill reading would've provided for you and others like you. The ability to articulate, to form punch lines, to use theater techniques to gather the masses and capture the attention of others. This is powerful and effective language. Enlightenment comes after you learn to gather and hold attention if you have the foresight to share what you've learned with the whole, thus creating education that results in the spread of knowledge. After communication takes a foothold amongst your brothers and sisters, your expression, the communication of your beliefs or opinions, would soon bubble to the surface.

Now, my friends, at that point you would have had the proper power and energy harnessed and at your disposal. Remember, all of this would've happened back during slavery if reading had been allowed.

## IMPROVED MEMORY:

Living a mentally active life is important, too. Just as muscles grow stronger with use, mental exercise helps keep mental skills and memory in tone. As a slave having a high-stress day, you would've had to keep your head on a swivel and your perception on high alert. In addition to all of this, you would still have to study and read when you finished working in the field for the day. With a developed memory, you would have too much to compare and contrast. The slave life would become finite to you in all aspects.

## IMPROVED WRITING SKILLS:

As the masses gained literacy, the ability to read and write would take a role amongst the hungry and frustrated. Maps, plans, and drawings of the slave plantation, guard duty, overseer's names and descriptions.

## HELPS PRIORITIZE GOALS:

Should be self-explanatory at this point in the game.

I've taken the liberty of giving a brief rendition of how deadly to the slave master and the slave system a group of literate slaves would've been back during those times. So, I have one question for you: What's your damn excuse now?

We live in a system in which free libraries still exist. Most are equipped with computers and free internet service. These libraries remain open fairly late. While there, no ropes are being brandished, no guns being shoved into your nostrils, no rawhide whips cracking for the slightest side eye.

The truth is, we as a people are not on shit! We've been turned into a docile subculture of useless eaters. This is not how I see things necessarily; it's how the rest of humanity views us.

What good is achieved by posting daily slave pictures of people that look like you and me? Does anyone do anything with that historical photo you post on social media? Is it going to create any jobs for the people, better infrastructure, manufacturing, skilled trades? We currently live in a spoiled present in which everyone owns a handheld encyclopedia called a smartphone. Millionaires do business with a single finger swipe.

What's your excuse again?

It's crazy that the same people crying about being broke acquire items much more expensive than what the richest once had. Smartphones cost as much now as a laptop computer did five years ago. We live in a time when looking rich get's you a woman because the success lines have been erased. The bar is now set so low that many are bored with the notion of trying hard without an immediate incentive.

You've been given various examples of what effort gets anybody willing to work at it.

## BUILD POINT:

Always remain ignorant of your own knowledge. Remember, learning is only effective if you can properly apply it to something.

Wisdom, on the other hand, will let you know just how limited your knowledge is compared to the grand scheme of things. Understand…our human lives are finite and fragile, which should warrant a certain level of beauty and appreciation from us. You must first start the process before you can develop a love for the procedure.

Think about it…

History provides examples of winning: Ali, Jordan, Oprah and many other success stories of the past and present shares a commonality. Each one of the strong, innovative souls I've described or mentioned all possessed a humble heart and a focused mind which allowed them to remain self-aware of goals both short term and long term as they navigated through the ebb and flow. Oprah didn't let abuse or any family dysfunction hinder her in her life's purpose. She focused on improving and continues to improve herself and those around her. Just think: She grew up being treated like shit. Now people refer to her as "the shit," a.k.a. the best.

Muhammed Ali used his popularity, fame, and platform to address & spark the beginning of conversations many Americans didn't want to face at the time. Some don't want to even today. Shit can take a long time. This was a man who changed his slave name, changed his religious beliefs, spoke his mind, said what he meant and meant exactly what he said. Ali received threats and vulgar insults thrown his way and still stood firm on his principles. For merely keeping his spine erect, attempts were made to force him out of a sport that he helped make more famous and lucrative.

In America, he who has the gold makes the rules. Still, it's important to remember that gold comes in many forms. This game isn't entirely based on material wealth or capital gains. Keep an ear open for golden advice you receive from a wise mentor or from a person who previously experienced the same or a similar situation as the one you're currently trying to muscle your way through.

## BUILD POINT:

Doesn't matter if you were born to be a superstar, somebody must mentor or coach you.

To bring out your full potential, you'll have to humble yourself constantly, be willing to start over from the bottom and work your way back up.

"The moment you feel comfortable you'll be wise to take stock of where you are and what you have going on in your life," said my grandmother Alberta, a.k.a. "Boss Lady."

Alberta accumulated multiple rental properties year after year, lived modestly, and is the sweetest lady you'll ever meet. Until you start talking business – then she transforms into a shark for the dough. She is not a Relator, nor does she know a bunch of slick real estate lingo to spit into your earlobes. She had the fortitude and foresight to say, "I have six children, and I'm going to be older a lot longer than I'm young." She proceeded to study, learn, and gather insight from people that were already doing what she was trying to do, as long as they had relative success at whatever it was, she was attempting herself.

## BUILD POINT:

Never take advice or instruction from anyone on any subject unless that person has had successful results themselves.

One thing that's awesome about the times we are living in now is the efficiency, speed, and methods we have at our disposal when it comes to using technology to gather information or using it to network with others. Next time you want to laugh, go outside and people watch. You'll notice that almost every person is buried in and consumed with the social media internet circus.

It's a sick joke being played on the masses – the notion of a "smartphone." The most used human device on the planet used to be called a "cell phone," and rightfully so. This device locks and paralyzes the users higher mind and if gone unchecked will dull the senses over time and produce an effect similar to what happens to zoo animals captured in the wild and raised in captivity.

The same person watching a viral video of a small kitten playing the piano will also proceed to cry broke but will never use the same cell phone to maximize or better their financial situation. We are past the days of playing sports or being an entertainer to earn a living or produce an above-average life situation.

There are more millennial millionaires being born and produced now than ever before. One advantage this new breed has over previous generations is technology. Despite having this great environmental advantage of the times at their disposal, they still out hustle and outwork the older so-called seasoned businessmen or businesswomen. What many people fail to realize about all of this is that opportunities are endless and available for everyone who's willing to put in the work and due diligence to thoroughly research and immerse themselves wholeheartedly.

## BUILD POINT:

Yes, it's tough to teach an old dog new tricks. Truth be told, it's almost impossible. Knowing the truth behind this age-old saying will enlighten you to a few things.

One: Always strike while your iron is hot, it's easier to create a spark.

Two: Time is undefeated, so it's always best to work with the clock, not against it. Time waits for no man.

Most anyone, even young men and women, can go on the internet and post exactly how they feel about anyone or anything going on in the world. Not just the day-to-day community happenings. You have modern new age boxing royalty such as

Floyd "Money" Mayweather who loves to talk trash and openly flaunts his fortune to the masses and various opponents on social media.

At the time of me writing this guide, the champ is currently 50-0. He's forever reaping the harvest of more famous boxers like Muhammad Ali, who planted seeds of boldness and success years before it was ever a money team. Floyd is no slouch when it comes to his craft. His often-chanted mantra is "hard work, dedication."

There is a reason celebrities can do and say what they want most of the time, even if they often offend a certain group of individuals. The backlash is short-lived, but why? Simple fact is that people always love a winner, even if they like to hate them. A top tier athlete or entertainer, for instance, can get hit with a drug or sex scandal and bounce back like it never happened.

An average person, however, would be dismissed easily or put in a cell to rot for the same damn thing. Exactly what is it? Could be the unapologetic swagger, the air of confidence, the charm, charisma. Perhaps it could be his or her tireless work ethic (grind). Despite all ridicule they may encounter, what makes them appear special to most onlookers?

Use the same confidence, mantras, habits, and routines of people you admire from afar because, at the end of the damn day, it's your own thought's, ambitions, love, fears, confidence, swagger that will take you along to where you want to be.

Understand that you can never be them. (You're never supposed to want to be.)

This is no attempt at brainwashing you to buying into a false fable. I'm merely giving you a broad perspective of how you can approach your life's purpose with an expansive, strategic, and steadfast outlook. Otherwise, you'll quickly fall victim like past generations that didn't have access to virtually unlimited resources.

## BUILD POINT:

You can never hit untouched heights if you aren't prepared for the long climb ahead.

What's the point of admiring someone who is very successful if you don't aspire to outdo them and pave your own success lane?

# BOSS BRICK NO. 22
## IT IS WHAT IT IS

---

"Bro…it is what it is…"

—De-Angelo, a.k.a Baby Bro

---

My little brother "D" would throw out a healthy ransom at my mental feet as a means to dead the debates we would have and still have to this day. This isn't a chapter about how my little bro is one of my most trusted advisers (fact). Nor is it about how I admire his hustle…the light so bright when he's turnt that you might need a visor (fact). "I'm just doing it for the benefits, big bro. All I care about is growing my business right now, to be perfectly honest," he would say.

By business, he is referring to his multiple real-estate investments, not to mention being a self-published writer/author. All accomplished before age twenty-seven. That might not seem like much of a big deal to you, but for an African American male from Detroit under the age of thirty to have financial assets, his own business, his own house, all gained without having children, took discipline, patience, and careful planning.

For any individual pissed off or feeling some way about the fact that I thought it necessary to add that this young man didn't have children when he acquired and accomplished the various things he did, I assure you it was never meant to be an insult to those that grind hard even though they have children. I'll explain my point.

Let's keep it 100% real: Raising a child until they come of age is a long and expensive endeavor. Unfortunately, for many people in the United States, having kids isn't really thought through seriously. What do I mean? The emotional tidal wave from society, culture, and family often overshadow the process.

You've heard the remarks: "You're not getting any younger;" "Who's going to carry on your name?" "Your eggs are going to dry up;" "What the hell are you waiting for?"

Most of the time when people have a child, it's not very well thought out. This is a fact. Point blank, if you're broke and struggling to feed or take care of yourself, you have no business bringing another human – born totally at the mercy of the surroundings – into this "movie" we call life.

I'm by no means an authority on anything, but simply put, I am a wave thrashing in the ether. I am a real friend without a filter. I only speak about what I know to be true by putting the examples and philosophies into the unkind flames to test the metal's worth.

## BUILD POINT:

I'd advise you to observe, learn to listen (most people wait to speak), and realize examples arrive in various forms. Be forever vigilant (keep your lantern lit), and always research for best results (learn as many angles to work as possible).

Maybe you never thought of the things I've been explaining

thus far…just remember it's no such thing as wrong, it all comes down to "perspective."

Check it out…

Mark Lino, an economist at the Center for Nutrition Policy and Promotion in Food and Nutrition, wrote in a January 2017 article for USDA about expenditures for children by families in 2015.

This report is primarily known as, "The cost of raising a child report." USDA has tracked the cost of raising a child since 1960, and this analysis examines expenses by the child's age, household income, budgetary component, and region of the country. Based on the most recent data from the consumer expenditures survey, in 2015 a family will spend approximately $12,980 annually per child. Remember, I'm talking about a middle-income ($59,200-$107,400), two-child, married-couple family.

Middle-income, married-couple parents of a child born in 2015 may expect to spend between $233,610 to $284,570, if projected inflation costs are factored in, for food, shelter, and other necessities to raise a child through age seventeen, not including the cost of a decent college education. Where does the money go?

For a middle-income family, housing accounts for the largest share at twenty-nine percent of total child costs. Food is second at eighteen percent, and child care and education, for those with this expense, is third at sixteen percent. Expenses vary depending on the age of your child. A more definitive route to take in figuring these costs would be the math on all expenses. Make skull notes to yourself, and always check your bankroll.

If you have children, you're not surprised that, the greater a family's income, the more that is spent on the child, particularly for childcare, education, and miscellaneous items. Expenses also increase as a child age. Overall, annual expenditures averaged about $300 less for children from birth to two years old and averaged $900 more for teenagers between fifteen and seventeen years of age. Teenagers have higher food costs as well as higher transportation costs, as these are the years they start to drive. Insurance is included, and a second car might be purchased for them.

Regional variation was also observed. Families in the urban northeastern states of Rhode Island, New York, Vermont, Massachusetts, New Jersey, etc., spent the most on a child, closely followed by families in the urban West, urban South, and urban Midwest areas. Families in rural areas throughout the country spent the least on a child— child-rearing expenses were twenty-seven percent lower in rural areas than the urban northeast due to lower housing and childcare and education expenses.

Most of your child's expenses are going to be subject to economies of scale, or basically large savings in your costs. (No wasted time or effort.) All gained by an increased level of production, i.e., your work ethic or capacity. That means, with each additional child you have or will have, there will be other expenses. For married-couple families with one child, the expenses averaged twenty-seven more per child than expenses in a two-child family. For families with three or more children, per child expenses averaged twenty-four percent less on each child than on a child in a two-child family. It's a crazy term the system likes to use and has used since the 1960s… the "cheaper by the dozen" effect.

The system often compares women to chickens hatching more eggs for the meat grinder. The system wants you to be driven by spontaneous passions, carnal natures, and instant gratification, as these things lead to snap judgments or decision making. After all, each additional child costs less, mainly because children can share a bedroom. Just keep having them and cram them one on top of another. A family can buy food in larger, more economical quantities by buying in bulk from a big warehouse superstore.

You know which ones I'm referring to. The clothing or toys can be handed

down (after all, they predicted all this shit using a reporting system implemented in 1960.) Finally, your older children can often babysit the younger ones.

This information was often numbing to my senses in the beginning, but I remembered… it's all perspective.

I'm not finished yet…

According to the 2017 Economic Policy Institute (EPI), "nearly half of families have no retirement account or savings at all." This includes saving vehicles such as IRA's and 401k's. The median for U.S. families is just $5,000, and the median for families with some savings is $60,000.

According to a 2016 www.gobankingrates.com survey, thirty-five percent, or roughly one in three of all adults in the U.S., have only several hundred dollars in savings accounts, and thirty-four percent have zero savings.

You might be asking, "What does this simple report actually prove?" Simply put, it proves that most Americans don't have a clue when it comes to discipline or careful planning. This is something my brother has always had at his disposal. He worked a 9 to 5 job to save up capital then started a small local landscaping business. While he was grinding physically, he stayed the course mentally as he read up on real-estate.

He studied 'how-to' guides on flipping houses, and of course, picked the brains of anyone that already played the game he wanted to play.

## BUILD POINT:

You'll never learn it all on your own. Focus on humbling yourself from the very start so that you can vigorously pursue knowledge and information about topics that interest you.

Approach people that successfully do the very thing you intend to do successfully. You're fighting time, and last time I looked, "time was and is undefeated."

My brother learned to use wisdom and hindsight to understand a universal law – the law of bossing- up. The formula is simple; most individuals think a boss is a person in charge of a worker or an organization. This definition is 100% correct but in reverse. See, the only person you'll ever be in charge of is your own damn self. The only organization you manage is the organization of your life painting. Now, that's a "boss," from my perspective.

Like Bob Ross, my little brother took his time, drew up a plan, and got up off his ass and got moving. Most people get caught up in the distant target, forgetting it takes patience and time to walk a thousand miles.

## BUILD POINT:

Let me remind you… you cannot see or hit your mark true if your base is

unstable.

Before a small home or any multi-billion-dollar structure is built, the soil, area, dimensions of the foundation, the climate and geography must be researched extensively. The final product is created within a specific framework that must conform. Even the placement of trees on the property is studied to determine which rendering will provide the building with the best natural lighting or shade.

I watched my brother go from having his bike, to riding the

bus to work for a year. And just like clockwork, his plans started to unfold.

He purchased a car with cash – no need for a note that's like having a friendly "bill" until it's not friendly. "D" went on to close on his first real-estate property. Six months of reading, grinding, saving, and writing down every move along the way gifted my brother with perfect setup opportunities. He's been moving, flipping, and sharpening his moves over the years ever since.

Rule of thumb in all of this … is plan your moves, check your bankroll, don't get in over your head, build a winning team, stay hungry. Children are a blessing, so reframe from cursing them with a hopeless lazy situation.

## BUILD POINT:

There will always be many layers to learn; the skin on the onion of life gets thick. Stay the course, no matter what obstacles present themselves.

If you plan on having even a moderate sense of success, you must strive to grow wise pertaining to your perception of all things. Be mindful of opportunities hidden in all things and situations. After all, you're going to be older longer than you're young.

Get me?

# BOSS BRICK NO. 23
## IT'S CAPITAL NOT THE COLLAR

"For to win one hundred victories in one hundred battles is not the acme of skill. To subdue the enemy without fighting is the acme of skill."

—Sun Tzu

A<small>T THE TIME</small> of this writing, the United States job market is over- saturated with complaining useless eaters. Meaning, since the wars and the prominent industrial age and space races ended, there has been an influx of depressed college graduates and college attendees.

During the 1940s through the mid-to-late 1970s schools were more industrialized than our current modern- day school system. For example, schools used to offer skilled trades to go along with general studies classes. This meant a student could graduate high school with skills in carpentry, woodworking, sheet metal welding, auto body, mechanics, plumbing/pipe fitting, and H-Vac, to name a few. We slowly traded in the practical means of creating personal or generational wealth by drinking the new "Kool-Aid" college to work a job.

We the people allowed the government to convince the masses to compete for a place at the crowded table of college graduates. A lonely place, indeed, for a skilled person without any friends or close allies helping to keep the coworkers afloat while at the job. See, in the corporate or mid-level skill jobs that exist today, companies strategically design the jobs to be as redundant or straightforward as possible. But, why?

If I make your position super simple to the point that even a monkey can do it (at least this is the mindset of management most times) with relative ease, how easy is it for me to dispose of you when I'm good and ready? Refer to my previous chapter where I talk about the influx of depression-related suicides. As the 2008 recession kicked into high gear, people invested heavily in higher education while, at the same time, entirely ignoring the benefits of developing practical skills which automatically lead to ownership. Unlike a job from which you can be fired or laid off, abilities can't be stripped from you; once you've got it, that's it.

These individuals quickly learned the hard way what happens when you don't know shit and can't do shit in a society that no longer requires or needs your limited skill set.

Allow me to draw a simple picture for you. Imagine being told your entire life that a piece of paper will save your life. No matter what, always pursue this piece of paper! You're told this piece of paper is a magical ticket that'll take you to untold heights of success, you just have to possess it.

Funny how, growing up, they say school is so important, only to find out its always been about human relations and "political science," along with some military science. After all, it's not always what you know; it's who you know. Individuals smile through school, knowing beyond a shadow of a doubt, they'll be college bound one day. You muscle through the lame classwork, redundant and non-practical homework assignments, tests, quizzes, lame lectures, midterms, and final exams to become a member of the 'I- have-a-degree-and-you-don't club.

You deal with all the hard work, politics, making friends with people you really can't stand, joining groups and community organizations, not because you are yourself very charitable, but because it looks better on your college application. After all of that work, long hours, and mental struggles, you finally graduate with an estimated $40,000 to $100,000 plus in college debt in your back pocket.

It's the perfect hustle; they (the system) make you pay for what you think is the best education you can have, then make you work the rest of your life to pay them back, with interest. For example, it's ten times harder for an eighteen-year-old to go to a bank right out of high school and get a small business loan for $100,000 so he or she can be an investor, entrepreneur, business owner, or a self-sufficient skilled tradesperson. However, he or she can be given hundreds of thousands of dollars in toxic debt by way of a college loan. This is the not-so-funny joke that many fail to realize.

I could paint a tapestry of facts and speak about the absurd policies left behind by the former United States President Bush, junior's administration. Most notably, the infamous No Child Left Behind Act. This policy, in a nutshell, would go on to help further cripple the practical, skilled, self-motivated I'd-rather-do-for-myself American attitude. We went from a country that loves to compete, show, prove, and produce the very best of everything to the opposite. However, long before that act was signed into law on any level, there was and has been a systematic attack on the psyche of the people, most notably the youth.

Perhaps if the NBA, NFL, or any of the major sports outlets

didn't pay adults so much cash to run, jump, dive, scream, and entertain the masses, everyday people would be more inclined to pursue more practical, versatile means of having and producing a wealthy living situation for themselves. Of course, this may seem like a rant to a lot reading this, but I assure you it is not.

I realize how the world is…

I'm a realist. Still, I'm not inclined to accept the status quo, and neither should you. I came to understand long ago that most Americans are more affluent than they realize. Ask yourself, why would a person living in a society in which you can gorge yourself on your favorite food while watching a so-called reality television show about the extreme cases of morbid obesity, laugh or feel sad about a person dying as a result of overindulgence? The last example was an obvious one, I know.

## BUILD POINT:

The system in which we currently live, work, and die was created to bring out either the very best or very worst in each individual. It's not set up for everyone to succeed and live abundantly. Everyone can't be CEO of Pepsi; however, nobody ever said you couldn't start your own soda company. That's possible for you to do since that's America in a nutshell.

Either you demand things, products, and services, or you become the supplier of products and services for those sitting still and demanding.

Our American society is built, runs, and thrives off the ignorance and over-indulgence of its citizens. Foreigners catch a bad rap because to the uninformed American-born person, "they come here and get everything handed to them by the government. They open businesses faster, build their communities up in quick fashion, etc., etc. blah, blah, blah." And so, the story goes.

Please allow me to hit you with a little bit of harsh truth and reality about how this country of ours really moves. The reason many foreigners fight tooth and nail to get to this abundant country is pretty simple – because the country is indeed fat, abundant, and full of opportunity. The incentive to boss-up is enormous when comparing those born in the United States to someone who is not. We have become spoiled, lazy, and dependent on our government or "big brother" for a helping hand.

We've lost our willingness to focus, hustle, and grind. There is too much focus on college education and not enough on ownership. Most "jobs" require very little education to carry out. Why?

Most corporations emphasize on-the-job training. A degree is only useful if you want to fight for a seat at a dinner table already crowded with elbows, fighting for crumbs. The government has pulled the greatest mind flip on its citizens. For example, learning practical skilled trades plays an important role in our economy and our society. Think about it; the sector touches almost every aspect of our lives, from the homes we live in, to the cars we drive, to the food we eat.

Real talk…

America, along with many nations on the planet, don't admit it enough, but it's painfully obvious that we depend on the work of skilled trades from skilled tradespeople. Why brainwash your children into seeking career opportunities that will have them working for another person? Hindsight will suggest they can create their own opportunities.

## IGNORED FACT:

People with practical skills are rewarded for their efforts with good pay. As an apprentice, a person working in the skilled trades can start making money right away because you 'earn while you learn.' The best part, though, is that as a tradesperson you get paid well doing work you enjoy.

Let's look at plumbers, for instance; the lowest twenty-five percent of apprentice earners reported pay of $36,050 per year or $17.33 per hour, while the highest twenty-five percent earned $64,790 per year or $31.15 per hour. Apprentice wages start at approximately half the rate of a journeyman (master) in most states and increase with experience and training.

Now, let's take a look at the dead-end jobs most teens are encouraged to work by society and even their families.

Fast food: Average total compensation includes tips, bonus, and overtime pay. A fast-food worker with mid-career experience, which includes employees with five to ten years of experience, can expect to earn an average total compensation of $19,000 based on ninety-eight salaries from across the board in that field.

See what I'm saying yet?

Now, I choose to explain the difference in pay between just two possible and real paths. The plumber has a real career, and the whole of society will always need a person with this skillset. Don't believe me? Well, let me know who you call the next time your toilet clogs up and overflows, or when your septic system is on the fritz.

The fast-food or retail worker is a laborer. A useless eater that can be discarded at will and easily replaced by a corporate machine. Why do you think you see different people at the window all the damn time when it's late and you go to get that burger and fries?

This is by no means any attempt to knock anyone working in the fast-food industry. Maybe you never had a real friend that wasn't afraid to tell you to your face that you were wasting time and energy on a dead-end pursuit. I'll never diss anybody feeding their loved ones or bringing a check home. That said, I can't stand idle while you or anyone else is brainwashed into accepting the status quo just because it's a safe bet. Safe, yes. However, the game you're playing is forever dirty, and you can never become clean lying down in a dirty bed.

## BUILD POINT:

You need to stop and think about what I've just explained to you. Use your high-dollar smartphone to look for a better job that will feed you and your family rather than watching cats play a piano.

Jobs are a dime a dozen, even those with benefits. No certainty exists of what tomorrow holds for you when you choose to punch another's time clock.

Conversely, spending the time to learn practical skills that nobody can strip from you should be your goal. As a result, you'll always have more say-so over the direction of your life. You should ponder this frequently.

I offer you real talk…

This system isn't created for everyone to have a good time, good day, or good life. Capitalism thrives off the rat race competition. This machine operates off the blood, sweat, and aggression of every participant moving within its maze. I, for one, am not here to advise you or anyone else what to do; only you know the answer to that question. However, I can offer you hardcore facts and perspectives so, at the minimum, you'll have adequate ammunition to fight this war more efficiently.

I realize I'm speaking to various groups with different points of view and traditions. I realized the truth of this before I wrote a single word of this book. Yet, knowing this compelled me.

Some will argue that it is impossible for everyone to be their company's CEO. I agree. We can't all oversee a single company or manage it. However, what exactly does that have to do with each of us being the boss and manager of our own individual lives?

You must see by now that herd mentality conditioning is a dangerous thing. This conditioning does nothing to enhance society as a whole. What it does do, and very efficiently, is create willing slaves, humanoid zombies that eat, sleep, shit, reproduce, work and die. Gone unchecked, in my view this situation will become worse over the next generations. We as a society must stop trying to place limitations on ourselves – in particular, the youth, by teaching them that college is the only hope for a fruitful life.

Right now, the United States has thirty million jobs that pay an average of $55,000 per year and don't require a bachelor's degree according to the Georgetown Center. People with career and technical educations are slightly more likely to be employed than their counterparts with academic credentials, the U.S. Department of Education reports. Also, these people are significantly more likely to be working in their fields of study. Skilled trades show among the highest potential among job categories, the economic-modeling company EMSI calculates. Please don't just take my word for it; look it up for yourself and you'll see the problem for what it is.

According to the report, current tradespeople are older than workers in other fields, as more than half were over forty-five in 2012. Looming retirement of these workers could result in significant shortages in their fields if many of us aren't proactive and willing to boss-up our own skill sets, as well as our children's.

I stated earlier in this chapter that so-called immigrants arrive in the U.S without a damn dime to their name. Fast forward five years, and they have a small family-owned business. I admire foreigners. They are not ashamed to grind and operate from a place of lack or temporary perceived inferiority. They realize very quickly that they have many resources at their disposal and strategize accordingly.

Meanwhile, even Americans that are considered to be poor live very abundantly compared to a person that immigrates to this nation, complaining to no end about wanting a new car, forgetting the fact that even if the vehicle they drive is considered to be a piece of shit, at least it runs. That same individual is angry at the Chinese laundry mat owner for feeding his or her family but will never even think about researching what it takes to open a business themselves.

We live in a time in which just about everyone in this country has access to the worldwide web through the smartphone. A pseudo college professor, maintenance manual, encyclopedia, and extensive reference guide, all in the palm of the hand. We've been so spoiled that we don't even realize the cruel joke of it all – which is that we have all the power in our very own hands.

Instead of blowing your hard-earned money on the latest smartphone, why not buy some books for your children to learn to code so they will grow up and design the next generation of smart technology?

Bottom line in all of this…

In this world, you're either on the top or bottom, either the buyer or seller. Which are you?

This is by no means a rant to prove the validity of skills over academics because we as a nation have to possess both if we intend to thrive and expand into the future. A humble, honest friend is all I am to those of you reading this guide with an open mind.

It would be best if you pondered this chapter objectively.

# BOSS BRICK NO. 24
## DON'T MAKE EXCUSES, JUST MAKE IT HAPPEN

"When there is no enemy within, the enemies outside cannot hurt you."

—African Proverb

O NE OF MY most interesting discoveries during my time walking this planet as a human is people's ability to become their own worst enemy. They do this despite the number of real, tangible enemies surrounding them at all times. I've mentioned this fact many times – I'm no guru or saint. I'm not perfect...only perfectly created. I say this as a precursor to the point we will eventually come to later in this chapter.

I've covered quite a few topics of discussion during our time together between these pages. Rest assured I'm well aware that I've managed to piss off many, inspired others, and even sparked a few with the stomach to digest my unique delivery of truth. However, while I'd love to keep slapping you with my redirect, I must leave room for your brain to absorb my words so you can come to have perspective and maybe a newfound approach to how you move through the twists and turns of this Western-driven life.

Yes, it's true that if you're born black in this country of ours, it often feels as if you were born with a target on your back. The air you breathe is heavy, and at times it feels as if you're an unwelcome guest at a house you practically built. As mortality rates currently go, black Americans are living longer, but racial gaps remain according to an article written in 2017 by the Center for Disease Control.

I know what you're saying if you're black -- what else is new? The article went on to state that the overall death rate for black people in the United States has declined about twenty-five percent in recent years. The bad news is that, although blacks are living longer, a racial disparity remains: The life expectancy of blacks is still four years less than that of whites. Younger blacks are more likely to live with or die from conditions typically found in older whites, such as heart disease, stroke, and diabetes, according to the report.

Now, I'm no physician or some big-I-little-you psychologist, but I can safely say this sounds a lot like a good ol' fashioned case of self-induced stress. I say self-induced for various reasons.

First, to add to the first point in the article, blacks have had a twenty-five percent drop in the overall mortality rate due to the lack of direct violence on our people by the system we seem to blame for every one of our issues.

I call major bullshit on our abundance of complaining about a threat that no longer exists. Yes, it's very accurate that police brutality exists heavily in urban black and brown communities. Still, how is that any different from any other time in America's bloody history, especially when it comes to how it deals with people of color? I'm merely saying there's a vast difference in the concentration of outward violence and persecution, a point many won't quickly admit. Police seem to target blacks more often… yes, seems so. However, we don't run or control the policing in our neighborhoods, do we?

## BUILD POINT:

We must encourage our youth to pursue the political arena on a local level and above. By doing so, we can work toward having law enforcement that is capable of showing the same level of empathy toward us as white officers clearly show their own brothers and sisters.

At one time in this bloody country, it was illegal to teach blacks to read or write. Education was used as a weapon. Slave masters understood that their social control of the slaves could not be based solely on physical coercion. Knowledge was power, and virtually all slave codes established in the United States set restrictions making it illegal to teach slaves to read or write.

The following is an excerpt from a North Carolina state-passed statute in 1830-1831:

"Whereas the teaching of slaves to read and write tends to incite dissatisfaction in their minds, and to produce insurrection and rebellion to the manifest injury of the citizens of this state:

Therefore, be it enacted by the general assembly of the state of North Carolina, and it is hereby enacted by the authority of the same, that any free person who shall hereafter teach, or attempt to teach, any slave within the state to read or write, the use of figures excepted, or shall give or sell to such slave or slaves any books or pamphlets, shall be liable to indictment in any court of record in this state having jurisdiction thereof, and upon conviction, shall, at the discretion of the court, if a white man or woman, be fined not less than one hundred dollars, nor more than two hundred dollars, or imprisoned; and if a free person of color, shall be fined, imprisoned, or whipped, at the discretion of the court, not exceed- ing thirty-nine lashes, nor less than twenty lashes.

"Be it further enacted, that if any slave shall hereafter teach, or attempt to teach, any other slave to read or write, the use of figures excepted, he or she may be carried before any justice of the peace, and on conviction thereof, shall be sentenced to receive thirty-nine lashes on his or her bare back. Be it further enacted, that the judges of the superior courts and the justices of the county courts shall give this act in charge to the grand juries of their respective counties."

Source: "Act passed by the general assembly of the state of North Carolina at the session of 1830—1831" (Raleigh: 1831).

Fortunately for many indigenous blacks born on American soil in these modern times, we don't have the threat of certain death from learning our ABC's anymore. Funny point of this little trip down memory lane is that despite such laws being taken entirely off the table, we as in the "indigenous blacks" don't take full advantage of this opportunity at our disposal. Disposal is a fine word to use to make my point since that's all we seem to do with the short list of opportunities we do have within our grasp. We treat a great many of them like trash.

I get it; I really do. All that built-up frustration generation after generation, beatings, hangings, rapes, and castration of the mind and often body parts will take its toll on a people.

Fact of the matter is, you're still here. While some racial extremists wish and pray for the old days to return, truth is…we will never go back to that era in history. Frankly, because that is what it is -- a time in history, and it's up to the current generation not to repeat a pseudo version of it during these modern times. Nobody has to grab you out your bed in the dead of night, drag you outside to a tree and string you up for all to see anymore. A lot of us won't get out of the bed every day on our own to build a better situation. What's sudden death compared to a slow painful one, huh?

I ask you, which one sounds better, and which sounds worse to you? Our ancestors were captured, beaten, and slain. The modern generation wants to complain and slowly dies of shame. The difference is painfully clear.

At the time of this writing, we are experiencing one of the greatest times in American history – the social media and information age. It is a technology-driven time period in which, essentially, a person can go from eating Top Ramen noodles to becoming a millionaire in the span of six months with the help of a smartphone and the internet. The reality that nobody wants to admit is that you don't need to have a college degree to achieve massive success in this country of ours.

An individual has to be able to do good business, and since the arena of business dynamics is ever-changing, all that is required of you to build a business from the ease of a smartphone is to be is adaptable and tech savvy.

Which brings me to another point…how do you expect to compete locally or globally if you're too lazy and afraid to learn something new and expansive? This goes well beyond reading and writing, but directly related to my point – some people risk life and the lives of their loved ones to activate their brain's hidden depths so that they can have a better future. So-called foreigners that immigrate to this country aren't racist toward blacks, at least not in the straightforward, cross-burning way the masses used to be within this country of ours. Immigrants are simply pro-whatever- they-happen-to-be. They practice hardcore "do-for- self-group economics; it's their overall bottom line.

The same goes for whites in the United States. They have historical ties to extreme brutality and racially-driven oppression tactics. However, this fact partly stemmed from a sense of self-preservation. Also, let me remind you that it took the mass majority of whites agreeing to enslave you for it to go down in the first place.

The brutal practice provided them free labor for 400 years; how else did the United States as a new nation become such a global economic powerhouse so quickly?

Blacks are quick to accuse other ethnicities of being heartless, selfish, and racist. However, it is often our lack of self-love and self-preservation that shoots us in the foot, further hindering any forward momentum we could otherwise have as a group if we ever found the nerve to think and move together as a unit.

CHASING A BAG"

A general slang term for…

hustling for money

grinding for financial success

focused on your business,

this term is a heavily-used popular phrase,

often said when a person is obsessively focused on getting some money.

## THE MIND GAME BEING PLAYED:

Allow me to paint a vivid scenario for you...

Imagine, if you will that you awake in a dark ally and see dark figures all around, screaming, crying, and shouting. Then the foul smell crawls into your nostrils...the smell of shit. Quickly, you realize you're standing knee deep in the foulest defecation, thick and dense like clay.

This wicked scenario is what it feels like being an African American born into generational poverty, lack, emotional instability, and defeatist mentalities. Even though the pain seems unbearable, you quickly realize there's a shovel, and to the left, a cylinder lodged into the shit. Congratulations, because you are actually aware of your surroundings enough to take note of these tools.

Tears slowly subside, and as hard as it is for you to take a breath, you acknowledge the smell along with your current immobile situation. The shovel is close enough for you to take hold of it with both hands. When you take hold, a rush of power (personal power) fills you. This is what it feels like when you finally decide to take your shitty life situation into your own hands and do something about it.

You proceed to strike this dense substance and grab a chunk, lifting it into the barrel. To your surprise, you notice after you place this shit into the container that the container has no bottom. It is almost as if the barrel represents the mind, and the shit, your imagination. More and more you dig until you can now move one leg and then the other until both feet are standing on solid ground. The air in your lungs is somewhat cleaner, breathing becomes deeper, and thoughts become sharp.

The sun creeps up over the horizon and terror grips you as you bear witness to your brothers and sister still stuck standing in their misery or shitty situation (immobilized by fear). Some can't reach out to grab their shovels (born with extreme disadvantages such as no father in the home, or dysfunctional family life situations), others got angry last night and snapped the shovel in half (frustration of the current state of things, or total loss of hope for a positive outcome). Some tried to eat their way out and choked on the shit itself, dying of suffocation (some try to adapt by feeding into the system's games and take on more shit than they can handle).

The point is, you might feel overwhelmed at times, but that has to be okay with you. Just because you were born into a shit-filled situation riddled with anger, frustration, death, prejudice, and violence doesn't mean all is lost. Maybe you are the one that broke your shovel in half. That had to be okay with you. Just know your arms and back are going to hurt more, but you still can dig yourself out and carve your own unique life path. Perhaps you feel overwhelmed at times, but this stems from an abundance of pride, a sense of "all I have, and all I'll ever have in this world is myself."

Let me be the first to say that that is utter bullshit and false. It has been my observation that all successful people are made successful by working together with other hungry individuals. The darkness of this exercise symbolizes our inner fears, that which is unseen but heard.

## BUILD POINT:

It is impossible to defeat an enemy that you cannot see, smell, or touch. The inner you, the one that knows all your deepest fears, lazy tendencies, and motivations works double hard to crush your spirit daily.

To make matters worse, if you fall asleep to this harsh reality, you'll gradually go into autopilot mode, slowly sinking into deep depression, laziness, and self-sabotaging behaviors that'll ultimately lead to misery, along with what I refer to as 'death before death.'

Understand me when I say this: we are only competing, fighting, and struggling against our own fabrications -- ourselves.

Excuses won't feed you, loved ones, or a community. Only effort, passion, and unity can achieve such things. Every other ethnicity has figured out this simple secret to getting ahead, and while we're behind on many levels, there is still time to bridge the gap and boss-up.

# BOSS BRICK NO. 25
## MOTIVATIONAL DOPE: EPILOGUE

"Outside the kingdom of the Lord, there is no nation which is greater than any other. God and history will remember your judgment."

—Haile Selassie

W E'VE TOUCHED ON many topics during our time together, you dig? I hope I've managed to spark a few brain cells with my low-key delivery. My true intentions will not be realized until a minimum of six months after these controversial, conversational bricks flood the street like motivational dope in the '80s. There'll be younglings showing more aggression for business and teamwork. Some children will shun parents that get in line with the new program.

These boss bricks can be snorted by all ages; however, it appeals most to the youth as they haven't been corrupted by history and distorted by views of how the world works. The youth still have their imagination and a healthy supply of willpower to scratch, fight, and bleed for what they want.

The cool thing about being a child is the fearlessness that comes with it. Remember back when you were young. Think back to the time when pain, exhaustion, failure, or death never crossed your mind. All of a sudden, you made the mistake of falling prey to a lesser family member or a lazy friend's words of discouragement.

Little by little, year after year, your will and energy chipped away until you bought into the illusion of being a so-called grown up. The so-called adults are really lost children; they are the slaves; the sheep being led astray daily by the soulless meat grinder we call adult society.

This is not a part of the book most will like; if you've made it this far, I have to commend you. At this time of conversing with you, I'm only in my thirties, still a relatively young man. I can tell you first hand, I've experienced the most success when I've refused to listen to society's views of what my life should look like based on where I was born, or the body I was born into.

For example, I knew a guy once, and for the sake of privacy, let's call him "T." He was an honor roll student and received over $15,000 in grants, along with 60,000 in credit cards his freshman year of college. T chose to max out the credit cards by withdrawing cash to buy pounds of weed, and he flipped the money. He then used the money to pay off each of his credit cards and proceeded to cancel and cut up each card after paying off the balance.

These actions accomplished three main goals: One, it provided him with working capital he didn't have. Secondly, it allowed him to focus on school full time without getting a minimum wage job that would ultimately eat up most of his prime studying hours. Lastly, and the best part of his plan, he built a strong credit history over the next two years which would translate into a strong credit score moving forward for all future endeavors.

Some of you are undoubtedly laughing and saying 'damn',

while a few see the method to his madness. Now, before anyone reading this tries to act self-righteous and pass judgment on my financial moves, let me remind you of a famous financial gangster by the name of Meyer Lansky, a man who according to many accounts (no pun intended), helped the La Cosa Nostra, the Italian-American mafia, amass billions of dollars through laundering money made from selling massive quantities of alcohol during prohibition. This was just one of the ways the mob amassed a fortune.

Like Meyer Lansky and every other true businessperson, T understood that when a need isn't being met, a high potential exists to capitalize and make a profit. You might say what T did at eighteen wasn't the same, and you are entitled to your opinion. Still, I choose to use my personal experience and perspectives as an example of how using your head and imagination can help you get ahead. Understand that T was still very immature at the time, but he would always allow his imagination to run wild, and his thoughts became very flexible.

To further add to my point, money laundering remained legal until 1986 when Ronald Reagan sponsored legislation that made it a federal crime. So, because the government couldn't track the mob's money, they were creating enough wealth to sway political influence in their favor. Of course, the government put certain things in place to avoid particular groups from becoming too big over time. There was also the threat of other minority groups using tactics to get ahead in the future. That's what our society does to every mind it can get its filthy hands on. This beast of a machine can and will inflict pain and aggression on anyone brave enough to challenge the status quo, or anyone brave enough to allow their inner child to thrive, unburdened by stress, fear, or defeatist redirect.

## BUILD POINT:

Always allow your inner child to live and thrive inside of you, as this is the side most feared by those that would see to it that you become a productive member of society, or in reality, a desensitized industrial slave.

We've touched on the weighty subject of slavery's ruthlessness and crudeness from the seventeenth century through the mid-eighteenth century. A strange part that often eludes most individuals nowadays is how slavery still exists; it's not only alive and well but thriving as we speak. To compound problems, the parents, teachers, and mass media outlets play the most influential role in priming the next generation for slaughter. For most people growing up in what society would label "urban" areas, the chance of being a part of the so-called American dreamer's club is slim, to say the least. At every turn, you're reminded of where you come from, as if you're doomed. Everywhere you look you see dirt, grime, and violence. You often learn aggression before you learn any manners.

Let's keep it real; for a lot of us, that was precisely our experience when growing up. As a kid, I had a few choices to thumb through. Could literally follow in the footsteps of my older peers and elders and end up in the same adverse situations, or worse. I could listen to all of my family members' negative, defeatist points of view and fall victim to my circumstances. Fortunately, I was blessed to have many friends from many different backgrounds since my mother would move us around quite a bit when my brother and I were young.

I'm a natural social being, and I analyzed everyone that crossed my path. What I learned shocked me; many of my friends came from neighborhoods more dangerous than mine. Despite that major difference in our worlds, their outlook on life and the future was far brighter than most kids our age at that time.

A simple fact that eluded me before I found my footing was just how vital your inner circle is; I refer to as my team.

I've had many teammates over the years. I got along great with some and couldn't stand others, but we all respected one another, regardless. They weren't afraid to go hard for their truth, much like me.

I've had the time, discipline, and patience to study many books about credit repair, stock trading, block chain technology, and branding. By age twenty-six, I made my first $100,000 in cash. Some of it was shoe box money, of course, but most of it was used to make stock investments.

I've owned homes in different states that I've flipped or sold at closings to a ready buyer for quick cash. I often had a saying while in my twenties: "If it was over ten, I was all in." I'm currently in my early 30's and very close to earning my first million. Very soon, I'll have it. Remember what I stated earlier – I'm no financial guru, money sage, or self-righteous show off trying to sell anyone a dream. I'm only a young guy that hustles hard and was unafraid of bumping my skull a few times to learn the hard way and find out the answers to some questions.

This book is my way of giving back, my way of trying to say '"thank you' and repay many of the people that gave me game, even when I didn't realize it at the time. These bricks of motivational dope I'm giving you won't solve all your problems; in fact, after reading this book, you might have even more questions that need answering. But I promise the questions you'll find yourself asking from this point on will be those that have a definitive goal behind them.

Promise you'll no longer accept what your family says as the gospel for what you can truly become and aspire to achieve for yourself. No longer will you be willing to settle for some makeshift existence at somebody else's table -- you'll be prepared to boss-up, do for self, and build your own table from scratch. This I promise you.

> "Give me an honest friend over a snake-blood relative any day of the week, and I can really do some damage"
>
> —The Builder

I've tried using various facts, figures, and real-life examples of how success is built, abused, and often destroyed. I purposefully left some subjects open for interpretation because your success or failure is ultimately up to you and what you choose to make of it. Let me make it clear that success and failure are the same; it just comes down to mastering the balancing act and having the scales remain in your favor for a sustained period that makes you successful.